A Simple Guide To
Chinese Ingredients
And Other Asian Specialties

Acknowledgements

Research and Administration:
Jennifer Louie

Research Contributors:
Deanne Dobler
Laura McEwen
Diane Onizuka
Susan Yan

Culinary Consultants:
Bernice Fong
Judy Lew
Jan Nix
Rhoda Yee

Special Thanks to:
Ginny Bast, Yvette Leung, and Gloria Pang
Stephanie Jan, Mami Nakamura, Tokie Onizuka, and Ying Woo

Graphic Designer and Food Stylist: Bernie Schimbke
Photographer: Charlie Frizzell
Typesetter: Ned Takahashi

Printed by Dragon Seed Publication (H.K.) Co.
Published by Yan Can Cook, Inc.
P.O. Box 4755, Foster City, CA 94404

 ISBN 1-884657-00-1

First Edition
9 8 7 6 5 4 3 2

Table of Contents

INTRODUCTION   4
A Wok In Chinatown   5

BASIC COOKING TOOLS AND TECHNIQUES   6
  Basic Tools and Equipment   8
  Basic Cutting Techniques   10
  Basic Preparation Techniques   11
  Basic Cooking Techniques   12

SEASONINGS   14
  Dry Seasonings   16
  Chinese Medicinal Herbs   21
  Sauces and Pastes   22
  Regional Chinese Cuisine   32

RICE, NOODLES, FLOURS, AND STARCHES   34
  Growing Your Own Vegetables   43

FRUITS AND VEGETABLES   44
  Fresh Produce   46
  A Dim Sum Experience   57
  Canned and Preserved Ingredients   58

OTHER TRADITIONAL INGREDIENTS   64
  Yin and Yang   70

SELECTED ASIAN SPECIALTIES   74
  Preparing Fresh Coconut Cream and Milk 87

ASIAN INGREDIENT SOURCES   89

INDEX   90

Introduction

Over the years, I have had the great privilege of introducing Chinese cuisine to millions of viewers of the *Yan Can Cook Show* and to many readers of my cookbooks both in this country and around the world. It has been a great pleasure for me to share this wonderful experience with all of you, whom over the years, have become a part of my family. In writing this book, I have decided to take a slight detour from my usual format of a recipe book. In fact, as you read on, you will soon realize that this book contains not a single recipe, and that it is a personal guide to some of the most common Chinese and Asian ingredients.

The variety of items found in Asian markets can be a formidable obstacle to someone who does not frequent these markets, as many packages are imported from Asia and do not have English labels. When a label does have English information, it is often misleading or confusing. Fresh produce and seasonings found in Asian markets may seem exotic unless you are familiar with their tastes and how to use them.

This book is written as a practical guide to bring along with you on your next trip into an Asian market. It is divided into five categories, according to how the items are commonly stocked in the market. Although a majority of the items are Chinese, I have also included plenty of other Asian products. For easy identification, each ingredient has a photograph as well as its Asian and English names.

I offer this book to you, as a small token of my appreciation for your continued support. I hope you will find it useful during your next venture into the rich and limitless realm of Asian cuisine.

A Walk In Chinatown

No matter how often I go to Chinatown, each visit is a new and exciting adventure. Perhaps I'll stumble upon a seasonal fruit or vegetable that's only available a few weeks out of the year, or I'll savor the sweet taste of moon cakes which symbolize the beginning of the Mid-Autumn Moon Festival.

Set aside a couple of hours so that you can experience the sights, sounds, and aromas that are only unique to this area. As you stroll from street to street, look at the many buildings with touches of traditional Chinese architecture and the bright red and gold-colored awnings with Chinese characters.

Stop by the produce stand and buy a bag of fresh fruits and vegetables. Walk by a seafood market and you will be amazed by the many different varieties of fresh fish and shellfish found in huge tanks. Stroll into a meat market and choose ducks and chickens live or dressed with head and feet intact. If you have a sweet tooth, try the bakeries which offer a selection of pastries that are usually less sweet and rich in comparison to western treats.

If you have a sudden urge for a snack, get the ultimate in Chinese fast food and pick up some barbecued pork or some other tasty treats at a Chinese deli. If you love pasta, drop by a noodle factory where a dozen types of wheat and rice flour noodles are made fresh daily. Thirsty? Walk in a tea shop and experience a tea ceremony. Peek into a fortune cookie factory and pick up a box of lucky fortunes.

By now, you must be hungry. It's time for a scrumptious dim sum lunch in one of the local tea houses where you can feast on several dozen varieties of delicious dumplings. If you ate too much and have a little indigestion, visit a medicinal herb shop where the herbalist will prescribe a soothing herbal tea from the thousands of dried herbs.

Your last stop should be to one of the grocery stores. With this book in hand, you can shop with ease and confidence. If you can't locate a particular item, simply show the store keeper the photograph.

Amidst all the hustle and bustle, get a feel for Chinatown's culture and people. Notice the Buddhist temples with their many religious offerings; the Chinese art galleries displaying traditional brush paintings and scrolls of calligraphy; and the curio shops full of traditional Chinese arts.

Take your time to explore and experience all that Chinatown has to offer. Every visit is bound to be different as Chinatown is always changing. One never knows what they'll find when walking in Chinatown, but it's guaranteed to be an exhilarating experience.

Basic
Cooking
Tools and
Techniques

Basic Tools and Equipment

The selection of cooking tools and equipment available to today's cook is truly remarkable. There's a finish, shape, and size of any piece of equipment to fit every cooking need.

You might think that to cook Asian dishes, you need a whole new set of fancy cooking utensils and equipment. Fortunately, many Asian recipes can be simply prepared with a wok, spatula, ladle, chef knife, steamer, claypot, mortar and pestle, and a few high-quality pots and pans.

While it's nice to have special-purpose utensils and equipment, you can adapt the pieces you already own to fit your needs. If you do need to make a few purchases, remember to always buy high-quality pieces. After all, you want these valuable utensils and pieces of equipment to last for a long time.

The Wok

The single most important tool of the Chinese chef is the wok. The wok, a concave bowl-shaped pan, is the most functional all-around cooking utensil. The wok can take the place of a dozen pots and pans, since almost any cooking method can be done in it from stir-frying to steaming.

Woks come in a wide variety of sizes and are made from a number of different materials. You can find some as small as 9 inches in diameter or as large as 24 inches for restaurants. Round or flat bottomed woks can be made from spun carbon steel, stainless steel, aluminum and stainless steel (often with copper sides and bottom), or hard anodized aluminum (with or without a non-stick surface). The traditional round bottomed woks can be used with a ring stand which sits on a gas burner. Flat bottomed woks are very efficient when used on an electric burner because of the increased surface contact with the heating element.

The key to successful wok cooking is the proper care of the wok. To season a new spun carbon steel wok, you should first wash it thoroughly with hot, soapy water to remove any protective coating applied at the factory. Dry the wok thoroughly, rub some vegetable oil with a paper towel evenly into the cooking surface, and gently heat the wok while continuously rubbing the surface with the paper towel (changing the towel as necessary). Continue this procedure until the wok begins to darken. This builds the first layer of a "seasoned" surface and will prevent food from sticking. To clean the wok, wash with hot water (with very little or no soap), dry well, and rub in a little fresh oil if it is not used daily.

Spatula and Ladle

The metal spatula is a multi-functional, long-handled tool that is curved to fit the sloping sides of the wok. The ladle is used along with the spatula to quickly toss and scoop the meat and vegetables as they are cooking.

The Chinese Chef's Knife

The Chinese chef's knife is as indispensable and multi-functional to the Chinese cook as the wok. The basic design of this tool, with its large, wide blade and slightly curved edge, is ideal for slicing, dicing, shredding, mincing, or crushing. Look for a Chinese chef's knife that is made of high carbon stainless steel, is well balanced, feels good in the hand, is easy to sharpen, and keeps its sharp edge well. After each use, wipe the blade with a hot, soapy cloth, rinse, and wipe dry. The Chinese chef's knife may feel a bit large and awkward the first time you use it, but go slowly while you develop your skill, and soon you will be slicing with ease. Most Chinese chef's knives are not designed for chopping through dense bones; for this job, use a real meat cleaver or let your butcher do it for you.

The Steamer

There are two types of steamers available, bamboo and aluminum. Stackable bamboo steamers allow one or more dishes to be cooked over a wok of boiling water.

Many Chinese chefs prefer the traditional bamboo steamers because their woven tops allow excess steam to escape without condensing and dripping back into the food. Wash bamboo steamers with hot, lightly soapy water, rinse well, dry, and store in an open shelf or cupboard.

If you don't have a steamer, you can use small cans (such as water chestnut or tuna cans with the tops and bottoms removed) as stands to hold heatproof dishes above the water in the wok. Or simply do it the old-fashioned Chinese way and place two pairs of chopsticks in a tic-tac-toe pattern to make a stand for the heatproof dish.

Claypots

These traditional earthenware pots, with their unglazed exteriors, are used for slow-cooking braised dishes. They come in many shapes and sizes and are mainly glazed in the interior. Be careful to never place a cold empty pot directly on the heat, or a hot pot on a cold surface as this may crack the pot. Any heatproof covered casserole is a good substitute.

Mortar and Pestle, Mini-Processor/Spice Grinder

The mortar and pestle, usually made of heavy stone, is a basic utensil in many Southeast Asian kitchens. It is used for grinding and pulverizing spices and herbs into fine pastes. Although the mortar and pestle is an excellent tool in extracting and releasing the aromas and flavors from the spices and herbs, the electric spice grinder or mini-food processor does the job almost as well and quicker.

Miscellaneous Tools

Along with the basic cooking tools and utensils, there are other tools which can be very useful in the kitchen, however, they are not absolutely necessary in producing a delicious and nutritious meal. The wire skimmer is used for lifting food out of hot water or oil. A few long cooking chopsticks are handy for turning and removing food while cooking.

Slicing

This technique is used to cut meat or vegetables into the desired size used in a recipe. Hold the food firmly on the cutting board, with fingers curled and perpendicular to the blade, and cut straight down with the knife.

Matchstick or Julienne Cutting

Cut the ingredient into thin slices, stack the slices, and cut vertically through the stacks, to resemble the size of wooden matchsticks.

Cubing, Dicing, Mincing

First cut the ingredient into long sticks, then cut across the sticks perpendicularly to make cubes of the desired size. Usually in recipes, cubing means about ¾-inch cubes, dicing about ½ to ¼-inch cubes, and mincing about ¹⁄₁₆-inch cubes.

Crushing

This technique is often used with garlic, ginger, or salted black beans to release their flavors. Place a garlic clove or a slice of ginger on the cutting board, then hold the chef's knife horizontally on top of the food with the blade facing away from you. Smack the broad side of the blade with the heel of the palm of your free hand to crush the food underneath. Crush black beans with the handle end of the cleaver.

Roll Cutting

This technique is used to cut long vegetables such as carrots or zucchini. First cut a diagonal slice at the tip of the vegetable. Then roll the vegetable a quarter turn, and cut again at the same angle. Repeat the turning and cutting until you reach the final cut.

Meat Cutting

To cut boneless meat for stir-frying, always cut across the grain (at right angles to the direction of the meat fibers) into thin slices. This ensures the meat will be tender after cooking.

YanCan Cook

Marinating

Marinating mainly adds flavor to meats, poultry, and seafood before cooking. Foods can be marinated from 30 minutes or overnight in the refrigerator. Some recipes may specify to drain the food or lift it out of the marinade; if it's not specified, a small amount of marinade can go into the wok with the meat. The small amount of marinade will evaporate quickly and add flavor to the dish.

Soaking

Many of the dried Asian ingredients, such as dried black mushrooms and fungus or dried shrimp need to be soaked prior to cooking. About 30 minutes of soaking time is usually enough. While the ingredients are soaking, you can prepare and organize the other items to be used in the recipe. You may also soak, drain, and refrigerate the ingredients the night before.

Toasting

This technique is used to release the flavor of ingredients such as sesame seeds or Sichuan peppercorns. To toast, place the ingredient in a small, dry pan and cook over low heat, shaking the pan frequently, until slightly darkened and fragrant. Small amounts of nuts can be toasted using this technique; however, larger amounts should be toasted on a baking sheet in a 350° F oven until golden brown.

Preparation

To cook Asian food successfully you should have everything cut and measured and ready to go before you turn on the heat. At first you may not be able to cut meats and vegetables into evenly sized pieces, but with a little practice you'll soon be cutting like an expert. Combine sauces and group piles of ingredients in a logical order according to the recipe directions. Read the recipe directions before you start cooking to get an idea of what you're about to do.

Stir-Frying

This method of cooking is the most common technique used in Chinese restaurants and in the home. It is called stir-frying because the food is kept in constant motion by stirring or tossing which ensures even cooking. This quick, simple process retains the flavors, textures, and nutrients of the food.

Organization is essential in stir-frying. Prepare the sauces and cut up all the ingredients before heating the wok. After everything is organized, place a wok or wide frying pan over high heat until hot. Add the oil and and the flavoring ingredients, such as garlic and ginger, and cook a few seconds to allow the flavoring ingredients to release their flavors into the oil.

The next step is to add the meat or seafood. Toss the food rapidly in the hot oil to seal in the juices. Meat and seafood are usually cooked, then removed before the addition of the vegetables. The leftover juices will help flavor and cook the vegetables. Vegetables are added according to their length of cooking time, with the denser or tougher in texture vegetables added first, followed by the smaller more fragile vegetables.

After the vegetables are cooked, the meat or seafood is returned to the wok. A sauce is then added to glaze the cooked ingredients. Next a cornstarch solution is added near the end of cooking to lightly bind all the flavors and textures.

Braising

This technique is commonly used to cook bigger, tougher cuts of meat which require a longer cooking time. Braising is basically a two-step process. First the meat is lightly browned to seal in the juices and to give a nice color. Then the liquid and seasonings are added. The wok or pan is covered and placed on the stovetop to cook for several hours. The meat will be very tender and succulent as a result of the longer cooking time.

Steaming

Steaming is one of the best ways to retain the natural flavor and nutritional value of fresh ingredients. It is also a very healthy cooking technique because it uses little or no fats or oils. To steam, bring water to a boil in a wok or wide frying pan. Place the food in a heat-proof dish and place it on a steamer rack above boiling water. Cover the steamer with a tight-fitting lid and steam until the food is done, adding additional water as needed.

Remember to be very careful when removing the steamer lid. Always tilt the lid away from you, so the escaping steam will not burn you.

Blanching

This technique is commonly used to quickly precook vegetables in boiling water. Bring a wok or large pot of water to a boil. Add the vegetables and cook for a few minutes, until crisp-tender or until the color turns bright. Quickly remove the vegetables from the wok and rinse under cool water to stop the cooking process. Blanching is also used to remove the metallic taste from canned vegetables such as bamboo shoots or straw mushrooms.

Roasting

In China, roasting has generally been a technique used in restaurants since most homes do not have ovens. In traditional Chinese ovens, marinated meats or poultry hang on a hook and cook over a wood-burning fire. This technique allows the air to circulate which results in a crisp exterior and a tender, moist interior. It is easy to duplicate this method in a home oven. Place the marinated meat on a rack in a foil-lined baking sheet. Baste the meat with the marinade or pan juices and turn occasionally to allow even roasting.

Simmering

This technique gently cooks food just below the boiling point in enough liquid to cover. Foods cooked using this method are generally tender, juicy, and flavorful.

Red-Cooking

Red-cooking is the technique where foods gently simmer over low heat in a liquid consisting mainly of soy sauce and sugar. The food takes on a deep mahogany-colored glaze. Red-cooked meats come out tender and juicy with a rich full-bodied flavor of the sauce.

Deep-Frying

Deep-frying is a cooking technique where food is cooked in a large amount of hot oil. This type of technique produces a crisp golden exterior and a moist interior.

It is important to deep fry the food in small batches because this will keep the oil at a constant temperature, and the food will cook evenly. When the temperature of oil drops, the food will become greasy rather than crispy. Remove the cooked food with a wire strainer or slotted spoon and drain well on paper towels.

Seasonings

Dry Seasonings

Brown Slab Sugar

(Cantonese) Wong Tong, Pin Tong;
(Mandarin) Huang Tang, Pian Tang
黃糖,片糖

As the name implies, brown slab sugar is a slab of brown sugar. More specifically, it's a combination of compressed layers of semi-refined brown sugar, white sugar, and honey. The thin slabs typically measure 3 to 5 inches in length.

Use a mortar and pestle to crush slabs into a manageable measuring size or place a few slabs in a plastic bag and crush with a rolling pin. When melted into sauces or added to braised meat dishes, the two-toned caramel-colored slabs add a rich, sweet flavor and a shiny glaze.

Brown slab sugar is found loose in bulk containers and in 1-pound portions wrapped in plastic packages. Store brown slab sugar in a tightly sealed container in a cool, dry place. It will keep for several months.

Chinese Five-Spice

Ng Heung Fun; Wu Hsiang Fen
五香粉

Back in old China, the number "5" was believed to have curative healing powers; that is why there were originally five spices present in this powder. Nowadays, Chinese five-spice may contain a few more ingredients. Five-spice includes combinations of cinnamon, star anise, fennel, clove, ginger, licorice, Sichuan peppercorn, and dried tangerine peel.

The wonderful aroma of the light cocoa-colored powder lends a distinct anise and cinnamon flavor to braised meats, roasts, and barbecues. Sprinkle Chinese five-spice and salt over pieces of roast chicken or pork to make otherwise plain meats more flavorful.

Look for Chinese five-spice in small plastic packages or in a jar in the spice section of most supermarkets. Store the loose powder in a jar with a tight fitting lid in a cool, dry place. It will keep for a year.

Chinese Hot Mustard

Gai Mut; Chieh Mo
芥茉

Chinese hot mustard is a pungent and fiery flavored condiment. It has a flavor somewhat like the Japanese wasabi, adding a clean tasting hotness to Chinese appetizers and cold meat platters. Unlike the fire from dried red chilies, Chinese hot mustard does not have a spicy bite or a lingering aftertaste.

This golden yellow sauce is usually paired with ketchup in Chinese restaurants and is served with deep-fried appetizers. Add Chinese hot mustard to chicken salad dressings and to dipping sauces for fresh vegetables.

A variety of Chinese hot mustards are available as prepared mustards and as dried powders. Store the loose powder in a jar with a tight fitting lid in a cool, dry place. Store an opened container of prepared hot mustard in the refrigerator. Both will keep for several months.

Rock Sugar

Bing Tong; Bing Tang
冰糖

Rock sugar, or rock candy, looks like a large, pale amber-colored crystal. It is made from a combination of refined and unrefined sugars and honey. This type of sugar adds a smooth, refreshing sweetness to foods unlike the cloying sweetness of common white sugar.

Rock sugar is used in braised meat dishes and in savory sauces. It contributes a lightly sweet flavor and glossy sheen. Rock sugar is also used to sweeten teas and hot and cold dessert soups. A 1-inch piece is about the same as 1½-tablespoons of white sugar. Place large pieces of rock sugar in a plastic bag and crush with a rolling pin to obtain pieces of a manageable measuring size.

Rock sugar is available in plastic packages and in cellophane-wrapped boxes. Store rock sugar in a tightly sealed container in a cool, dry place. It will keep for several months.

Salted Black Beans

Dou See; Tou Shih
豆豉

Black beans which have undergone a lengthy fermentation process are called salted, preserved, or fermented black beans. These little salt-speckled black beans lend a distinctly pungent, almost smoky flavor to cooked foods.

To use, gently rinse whole beans under running water and lightly crush or coarsely chop. For a more pungent flavor, mince the beans to a smooth paste. Add minced garlic to give the paste a savory punch.

Salted black beans come packaged in plastic bags. Buy beans that feel somewhat soft through the bag and do not look dried out. You may find them in cardboard cartons with the added flavors of citrus peel or ginger. Store all varieties of salted black beans in separate jars with tight fitting lids in a cool, dry place. All varieties will keep for a year.

Sichuan Peppercorns

Fa Tziu; Hua Chiao
花椒

Contrary to popular belief, Sichuan peppercorns are not related to common black peppercorns. These dried reddish brown bits are actually berries that have a woodsy fragrance. Sichuan peppercorns leave a pleasantly numbing feeling in the mouth, rather than a spicy, hot, burning sensation.

Sichuan peppercorns are used in many stir-fried and red-cooked dishes that are typical throughout the Western regions of China. They are also one of the spices used in Chinese five-spice. To bring out their distinctive aroma and flavor, toast a few handfuls in a dry frying pan over low heat until fragrant. Use peppercorns whole, crush in a mortar and pestle or spice grinder to a fine or coarse powder.

Sichuan peppercorns are available in plastic packages. They may also be referred to as red or wild pepper, but don't get these confused with common crushed red pepper flakes which have an entirely different taste. Store peppercorns in a jar with a tight fitting lid in a cool, dry place. They will keep for several months.

Star Anise

Bark Gog; Pa Chiao
八角

You can't miss star anise — nothing else in the world looks like it. Each 1-inch star has eight points and each point contains a shiny, mahogany-colored seed. Star anise has a distinct spiced licorice flavor that compliments both meats and poultry in red-cooked and barbecued dishes.

It is most commonly used to make rich braising sauces and stews. When used as a whole spice, star anise is not eaten. It is only used as a flavoring agent and is often placed in a spice bag which is removed before serving. Ground star anise is used to make Chinese five-spice and other flavorful powders and dipping sauces.

Look for whole and ground star anise in plastic packages and in small jars. It is impossible to find a bag of star anise with only whole pods which contain eight points. Nevertheless, eight broken points still equal one whole pod. Store whole and powdered star anise in separate jars with tight fitting lids in a cool, dry place. They will keep for several months.

Tangerine Peel, Dried

Guor Pay; Kuo Pi
果皮

Believe me when I tell you that a dried tangerine peel can make braised dishes, soups, and sauces wonderfully aromatic with a light citrus flavor. If you like citrus fruits, this gnarled, brittle, rusty orange-colored peel will be a sure favorite.

Before using, soak dried tangerine peel in warm water until softened. Scrape the underside with a table knife to remove the bitter white portion of the peel. Leave the peel whole or tear into quarter-size pieces before adding to braised dishes, stews, and soups. For use in stir-fries, dim sum fillings, and congee (Chinese rice porridge), cut the peel into julienne strips or finely chop.

Dried tangerine peel is available in plastic packages. If dried tangerine peel is not available, use dried orange peel. You can substitute one for the other in most dishes. Once opened, store dried peel in a jar with a tight fitting lid in a cool, dry place. It will keep for several months.

Chinese Medicinal Herbs

In China and many other Asian countries the use of herbal medicine is a professionally recognized medical practice and legitimate form of health care. It is a practice based on obtaining a balance between one's yin and yang forces. It is believed that when these two forces are not in equilibrium illness occurs.

Herbs are prescribed to patients to reestablish a balance between yin and yang. The herbs are most often obtained as dried pieces, ground powders, or pills. Some herbs are strictly used for medicinal purposes. Others, such as those listed below, are traditional seasoning ingredients which make flavorful contributions to foods as well as provide healing powers.

Black Fungus and Dried Black Mushrooms have a slightly salty, musky flavor. They are used to stimulate the immune system, promote blood circulation, and lower cholesterol.

Chinese Jujubes are reddish brown fruits which are usually found dried or preserved. They are not only savored for their sweet taste but also to treat anxiety, insomnia, and dizziness.

Cinnamon Bark is usually used in soups and is not difficult to recognize. As the name implies, its physical appearance looks quite similar to bark. Cinnamon bark is only used as a flavoring agent and is not eaten. It is used to stimulate digestion, respiration, and blood circulation.

Dried Tangerine Peels add a mildly spiced citrus taste to soups and teas. Not only are they used to relieve coughing, hiccups, and nausea but also to stimulate the appetite and aid digestion.

Ginger is a mildly spiced root which is known to relieve coughing, nausea, and dizziness. It is also used to aid digestion.

Ginseng is known as a panacea to Chinese herbalists. It comes in many forms — powder, capsules, whole, sliced, and in concentrated extracts. It's generally used to cleanse the blood, and as a stimulant and aphrodisiac. Ginseng is also used to treat anemia, nervous disorders, fevers, excessive sweating, and forgetfulness.

Lemongrass is a fragrant herb which is used to make flavorful teas, soups, and savory pastes. It is known to induce sweating.

Lily buds are often purchased in dried form. These 2 to 3 inch-long brown strands have a delicate musky, sweet flavor. Lily buds are used as a vegetable and as a garnish in stir-fried dishes. They are used as a tonic and sedative and are known to treat coughing and lung disorders.

Lychee is a popular Chinese fruit which is most desirable in its fresh form. It has a delicate sweet flavor and is known to help treat coughs, anemia, and fatigue.

Sauces and Pastes

Barbecue Sauce

Tza Siu Jeng; Cha Shao Chiang
叉燒醬

Barbecue sauce is made from fermented soy beans, vinegar, tomato paste, chili, garlic, sugar, and other spices. It has a thick jam-like consistency and a sweet and spicy taste. This bright reddish brown sauce gives the appealing color and flavor to Chinese barbecued spareribs and barbecued pork found at your local Chinese deli.

Use barbecue sauce as you would popular American barbecue sauces for marinating, basting, or as a dipping sauce for meats and poultry. Its sweet and spicy flavor will enhance any barbecue from roasted meats to grilled vegetables.

Barbecue sauce is available in jars. Don't confuse this barbecue sauce with Southeast Asian satay barbecue sauce. They are both used as barbecue sauces, but satay sauce is made from dried fish, dried shrimp, and other seasonings. Refrigerate an opened jar of barbecue sauce. It will keep for a year.

Black Bean Sauce

See Tzup Jeng; Shih Chih Chiang
豉汁醬

Although preparing salted black beans for sauces and stir-fries is quite easy, it is even faster to make black bean dishes with prepared black bean sauce, a ready-to-use sauce made of salted black beans and rice wine. Depending on the variety, garlic and hot chilies may be added.

All you have to do is add the prepared sauce to stir-fries and sauces and heat through. It is a super time-saver for appetizers and fast meals. It is a simple no-fuss way for cooks to introduce themselves to salted black beans with guaranteed results.

Prepared black bean sauce is available in various sized jars. Refrigerate an opened jar of black bean sauce. It will keep for a year.

Brown Bean Sauce

Mor See Jeng; Mo Shih Chiang
磨豉醬

Brown bean sauce is made from whole or ground fermented soy beans. As with most fermented soy bean products, it has a salty, bean-like flavor and somewhat thick consistency. Those that are thicker and have a greater proportion of unground soy beans are referred to as pastes. Whole and ground bean sauces and pastes are used interchangeably; the choice depends on availability and the desired appearance of the final product.

Use brown bean sauce or paste in braised meat dishes and as the main flavoring ingredient for steamed fish and vegetarian bean curd. Brown bean sauce with the addition of fiery hot chilies is called hot bean sauce or paste. It is a cross between brown bean sauce and chili sauce. Use it when a spicy, mildly hot flavor is desired.

Most varieties of brown bean sauce and paste are available in various sized cans and jars. Transfer the contents of an opened can to a jar with a tight fitting lid. Refrigerate opened jars of brown bean sauce and paste. They will keep for a year.

Chili Oil

Laut You; La You
辣油

This hot, reddish orange oil is made by infusing the heat and flavor of whole dried red chilies or crushed red pepper flakes into oil. It is used as a flavoring agent in cooking and as a table condiment for those who like to add a spicy bite to any food. Be careful; this stuff is hot and dangerous! Start off with one or two drops, then taste the food before adding more.

Add chili oil anytime you want to add a fiery hotness to your food. Add a few drops to stir-fries just before serving or make a dim sum dipping sauce by mixing chili oil with soy sauce.

To make homemade chili oil, heat a cup of oil until hot and add several tablespoons of crushed red pepper flakes. Shut off the heat, let the oil stand until cool, and then transfer the contents to a jar with a tight fitting lid. Store the chili oil in a cool, dry place for up to several months.

Chili Paste

Laut Tziu Jeng; La Chiao Chiang　辣椒醬
(Vietnamese) **Tương Ớt**

There's not much to say about chili paste
except that there are millions of different
varieties ranging in degree of hotness, flavor, and consistency. Most are made from a
blend of fresh and dried chilies and vinegar.
Depending on the country of origin, different seasonings are added to give each a
unique flavor. Some additional ingredients
include garlic, ginger, soy beans, and
sesame oil, to name only a few.

Choosing which paste to use is largely a matter of preference. For starters add Chinese
chili paste to your favorite stir-fry during the last minute of cooking. Try Thai sweet chili
sauce as a condiment to roast chicken. Use flaming red Vietnamese chili sauce to season
noodle soups. Try them all and adjust the amount of chili paste according to your taste.

Most Asian markets sell an assortment of popular chili pastes and sauces from different
countries. Start out by buying a small jar or bottle. Remember, a little goes a long way.
Refrigerate opened jars and bottles. They will keep for a year.

Fermented Bean Curd

Fu Yeu; Fu Ru
腐乳

Fermented bean curd is a soft and creamy
curd with a smooth, thick custard-like texture. The small cubes have a mildly pungent, wine-like aroma. There are two main
types of fermented bean curd, each having
many variations of the original. White varieties have sesame oil, rice wine, or chili
added. Red varieties are flavored with red
rice, rice wine, chili, or rose essence.

The red variety of fermented bean curd gets
its bright crimson red color from the natural oils of annatto seeds. Its wonderful color
and flavor enhances stews and clay pot casserole dishes, especially those that contain
chicken, pork, or duck. The somewhat saltier white fermented bean curd is often used to
season leafy green vegetables or is served as a condiment on the side of other dishes.

Choose jars which have pieces that shift with the motion of a moving jar. These jars contain
the most flavorful bean curd as they have been properly fermented and ripened. Refrigerate
opened jars for up to several months.

Hoisin Sauce

Hoi Seen Jeng; Hai Hsien Chiang
海鮮醬

A robust combination of fermented soy beans, vinegar, garlic, sugar, and spices is the basis for hoisin sauce. This thick, granular sauce has a spicy-sweet flavor that compliments many dishes. Its deep, rich reddish brown color accents American roasts as well as Asian stir-fries and barbecues. A sauce similar to hoisin sauce is chee hou sauce which has a spicier flavor.

Hoisin sauce often accompanies crepe-like Mandarin pancakes or steamed buns which are served with Mu Shu and Peking Duck dishes. Use hoisin sauce or chee hou sauce as a base for creating savory barbecue sauces and dipping sauces for meats and poultry.

Hoisin sauce and chee hou sauce are available in various sized bottles and jars. Refrigerate opened bottles and jars. They will keep for a year.

Oyster-Flavored Sauce

Hou Yeo; Hao You
蠔油

Oyster-flavored sauce is a thick, dark brown all-purpose seasoning sauce made from oyster extracts, sugar, seasonings, and cornstarch. It has a distinct sweet-smoky flavor that goes well with practically any meat and vegetable combination.

Oyster-flavored sauce is one of the most common ingredients in Cantonese cooking. In Chinese home-style cooking, oyster-flavored sauce is drizzled over simple dishes such as steamed Chinese broccoli and savory custard eggs. Its rich flavor and deep color will enhance the taste and appearance of any stir-fried dish or fried rice. Use oyster-flavored sauce as a dipping sauce for roast pork and chicken.

There are now a few variations of oyster-flavored sauce available in Asian markets, including hot and vegetarian style sauces. **Lee Kum Kee's** oyster-flavored sauce is possibly the best available. Refrigerate an opened bottle of oyster-flavored sauce. It will keep for a year.

Plum Sauce

Suin Mui Jeng; Suan Mei Chiang
酸梅醬

Plum sauce is made from salted plums, apricots, yams, rice vinegar, chilies, sugar, and other spices. It is a light amber sauce with a sweet-tart flavor and a chunky jam-like texture. Many restaurants serve plum sauce with roast duck and other barbecued meats. On the east coast of the U.S., some Chinese restaurants make their own special blend called duck sauce and serve it with barbecued duck.

There are many brands of plum sauce which differ in composition, taste, and texture. Try them all — you may find that you prefer a particular sauce with a specific dish. Plum sauce is delicious served with deep-fried appetizers and roasted meats.

Plum sauce is available in jars, bottles, and cans. Refrigerate jars and bottles after opening. Transfer the contents of an opened can to a jar with a tight fitting lid and refrigerate. All will keep for a year.

Rice Vinegar

Bok Tzo; Pai Tsu 白醋
(Japanese) Yonezu 米酢

Compared to distilled white vinegar, rice vinegar is milder, less pungent, and sweeter in flavor. Popular Chinese and Japanese rice vinegars range in color from clear or slightly golden to rich amber brown. Seasoned Japanese rice vinegar, sweetened with sugar, is also available.

Use rice vinegar to make sweet and sour dishes or to season vegetable dishes and salad dressings. For quick sushi rice, toss hot cooked medium-grain rice with seasoned rice vinegar. Use light and refreshing rice vinegar as you would other vinegars.

Many types of Chinese and Japanese rice vinegars are available in bottles. Store all varieties in a cool, dry place. They will keep for several months, but will lose flavor and intensity over time.

Rice Wine

Mike Tziu; Mi Chiu
米酒

Rice wine is the product of fermented glutinous rice and millet. The resulting amber liquid is aged 10 to 100 years to achieve its rich full-bodied flavor. Shao Hsing, a city in Eastern China, produces some of the better quality wines which are often specifically called for in Chinese cookbooks.

To retain its delightful aroma during stir-fry cooking, add rice wine just before serving. When braising or clay pot cooking "drunken" dishes, the mildly acidic rice wine is used not only for flavor but also to help tenderize tough cuts of meat.

Asian markets sell a number of rice wines of various origins and grades of quality. The price is usually indicative of the quality — so a bigger price tag means a better quality wine. When rice wine is not available substitute dry sherry or Japanese sake. Store rice wine in a cool, dry place. It will keep for several months.

Sesame Oil

Ma You; Ma You 麻油
(Japanese) Goma-Abura ごま油

Chinese and Japanese-style sesame oil is a dark amber oil pressed from toasted sesame seeds. Don't confuse this sesame oil with the clear, cold-pressed sesame oil sold in many health food stores. Unlike other oils which are used for cooking, sesame oil is used in small amounts solely as a flavoring agent.

Sesame oil adds a wonderful aroma and nutty taste to a variety of marinades and salad dressings. It is often added during the last minute of cooking soups, braised, and stir-fried dishes to preserve its aroma. For a tasty quick snack, add a few drops of sesame oil to a bowl of pasta and toss with slivers of carrots and green onions.

The better quality sesame oils are found in Asian markets and are labeled as 100 percent pure. Many companies blend sesame oil with soy bean oil which dilutes its nutty flavor. Store sesame oil in a cool, dry place for up to several months.

Sesame Paste

Tzee Ma Jeng; Chih Ma Chiang
芝麻醬

Sesame paste is made from toasted white sesame seeds. Like homemade peanut butter, it is similarly thick with a roasted, nutty taste and aroma. Ranging from golden brown to light gray brown, it is a common ingredient in Sichuan cooking.

Use sesame paste whenever a nutty flavor is desired. To use, discard the oil layer and remove the needed portion of paste. You may need to add a bit of fresh oil or water to soften the paste before adding it to dressings, sauces, and marinades. Middle Eastern tahini, made from untoasted white sesame seeds, or peanut butter mixed with sesame oil are acceptable substitutes when sesame paste is not available.

Sesame paste is available in jars. After opening, replace the protective oil layer with fresh oil. This will help prevent the paste from drying out. Refrigerate an opened jar of sesame paste. It will keep for several months.

Shrimp Sauce

Ha Jeng; Hsia Chiang 蝦醬
(Thai) Kapi น้ำเคย

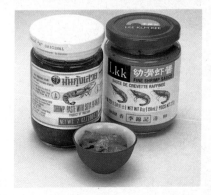

Shrimp sauce is a seasoning made from salted fermented shrimp. This pinkish gray sauce has a somewhat strong odor reminding me of past days spent fishing. Nevertheless, it is still a necessity in traditional Chinese and Southeast Asian cooking and holds a special spot on my pantry shelf.

Once shrimp sauce is cooked the pungent odor disappears, leaving a salty, mellow, fish flavor that goes well in fried rice, stir-fried leafy green vegetables, and savory clay pot casserole dishes. Shrimp paste is the sun-dried version of shrimp sauce. To use, cut a thin slice from the brown brick and pan-fry before adding to Southeast Asian curry pastes and sauces. One portion of the dried paste is about equal to two portions of the sauce.

A variety of Chinese and Southeast Asian shrimp sauces and pastes are available in bottles and jars. Refrigerate opened containers of shrimp sauce for up to a year. Store dried shrimp paste bricks in a tightly sealed container in a cool, dry place. They will keep for several months.

Soy Sauce

Jeng Yeo; Chiang You 醬油
(Japanese) Shouyu しょうゆ

No Chinese kitchen is complete without soy sauce. It gives most Chinese dishes their characteristic flavor and rich brown color. Many regions throughout China produce their own versions of soy sauce reflecting the tastes of that particular region. Although they may differ in color, aroma, and flavor, they are all made from the same basic ingredients — soy beans and wheat, using the same basic natural fermentation process.

Soy sauce is traditionally used for marinating, seasoning stir-fry sauces, braising liquids, roasting glazes, and salad dressings. It is a popular dipping sauce for roast meats and dim sum. Many home cooks as well as restaurant chefs use **Kikkoman** soy sauce which is consistently of superior quality. It is sweeter and less salty in comparison to most Chinese brands which are not only stronger and heavier tasting but also inconsistent in quality and vary in flavor from brand to brand. Mushroom-flavored soy sauce is another option for times when you want to add a light mushroom flavor and a rich dark color to your dishes.

Soy Sauce, Reduced Sodium

Dei Yim Fen Jeng Yeo
Ti Yan Fen Chiang You
低鹽份醬油

With today's interest in special dietary needs and health, some cooks prefer to use reduced sodium or lite soy sauce. Most lite soy sauces have an approximate 40 percent sodium reduction. This seems to be the soy sauce of choice for those who need or wish to reduce their total intake of sodium.

Though it tastes less salty, lite soy sauce has a rich flavor. Use it in preparation and cooking as you would regular soy sauce.

Because lite soy sauce has less sodium, it is more susceptible to spoilage and must be refrigerated after opening. It will keep for several months.

Soy Sauce, Dark

Lo Ceo; Lao Chou
老抽

Because of the addition of molasses, dark soy sauce is characteristically thicker, darker, sweeter, and more full-bodied in flavor than regular soy sauce. It is used when a richer flavor and a deep mahogany color are desired. Shanghai red-cooked meats and stewed dishes characteristically use dark soy sauce.

If you are not sure you are buying dark soy sauce, hold the questionable bottle of soy sauce and a bottle of known regular soy sauce upside down. Turn the bottles right side up and watch the soy sauce run down the neck of the bottles. Dark soy sauce will coat the bottle neck heavily and will slowly run down the sides of the bottle. Regular soy sauce will drain quickly with little visible residue.

Use regular **Kikkoman** soy sauce if dark soy sauce is not available. Dark soy sauce is not interchangeable with thin soy sauce, although they are often used in combination. Store opened bottles of dark soy sauce in a cool, dry place for up to several months. If you are a slow user, refrigerate dark soy sauce for up to a year.

Soy Sauce, Thin

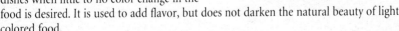

Seng Ceo; Sheng Chou
生抽

Thin soy sauce, also labeled as light soy sauce, is characteristically lighter in color, saltier in flavor, and thinner in consistency than regular soy sauce. It is not the same as reduced sodium soy sauce as the name might imply. Use regular **Kikkoman** soy sauce if thin soy sauce is not available.

Thin soy sauce is used as a marinade and to season vegetable, fish, shellfish, and poultry dishes when little to no color change in the food is desired. It is used to add flavor, but does not darken the natural beauty of light colored food.

In regards to all types of soy sauces, always choose those that are naturally brewed. Avoid buying synthetic, chemically hydrolyzed, or artificially colored soy sauces. Store all soy sauces, except for reduced sodium soy sauce, in a cool, dry place. Regular, mushroom-flavored, dark, and thin soy sauces will keep for several months but will naturally darken and become more concentrated over time. Refrigerate soy sauce if using the reduced sodium variety or if you are a slow user.

Sweet Bean Sauce

Tim Min Jeng; Tien Mien Chiang
甜面醬

Sweet bean sauce is made from fermented soy beans and sugar. Having a range of consistencies from thin to thick, sweet bean sauce may also be called a paste. Its salty-sweet taste makes this deep brown sauce a favorite among Hunan and Sichuan chefs.

Add sweet bean sauce to marinades or use to season stir-fried meats and poultry. Combine it with your favorite chili sauce to make a tasty dip for roast meats or add sesame oil and a little more sugar to make a condiment for Peking Duck and Mu Shu dishes.

Sweet bean sauce and pastes are available in cans and jars. Don't confuse this sauce with Chinese and Japanese sweet red and black bean pastes. Sweet red and black bean pastes are made from red and black beans and are used to fill a variety of savory and sweet treats. Transfer the contents of an opened can to a jar with a tight fitting lid and refrigerate. It will keep for several months.

Regional Chinese Cuisine

Among the world's great cuisines, the regional cooking of China is perhaps the most difficult to classify. Because many parts of China are isolated, the regional styles of cooking are as different as its dialects. Over the centuries, certain special dishes from one region have been adopted and adapted in other regions. Most Chinese cooks are notably inventive and flexible due to the availability of ingredients, and new dishes and foods are constantly being incorporated into each regional cuisine. For simple identification, we will only discuss the four better-known culinary regions.

The Northern School — Beijing or Peking
Beijing, home of the Imperial courts for many centuries, is the political and cultural center of China. Sophisticated menus influenced by the Imperial Court and its lavish banquet-style dining, produced an unusually refined style of regional cooking which drew cooking ideas from all over China.

Commonly called Beijing or Peking-style, the cooking of this region is characterized by tangy sweet and sour sauces and the famous technique of preparing Peking Duck. Interestingly, this style of cooking includes many Mongolian dishes due to its northwest bordering neighbor, Inner Mongolia. Best known are the Mongolian Hot Pot, a cooking method similar to fondue, and lamb dishes which have become popular throughout China.

The northern region is far too harsh an environment to grow rice. Oats, wheat, and soy beans are the area's primary crops. Noodles, dumplings, rolls, and breads that accompany meals are usually made from one of these three staples. Seasonings, of course, are an important part of the northern cuisine. Particularly useful are garlic, ginger, and green onions.

The Southern School — Guangzhou or Canton

Guangzhou is the capital city of Guangdong province which is located on the southern tip of China. It has a mild, tropical climate and abundant rainfall, which makes it a rich agricultural region. Guangzhou is a bustling port city long known as a culinary center drawing exotic ingredients from all around the world.

The Cantonese kitchen is characterized by this vast choice of endless combinations of ingredients and textures. The southern region is also famous for its tea houses, which feature a variety of dim sum, tantalizing bite-size snacks (see page 57). Southern chefs fry, roast, steam, saute, barbecue, and braise an astounding array of meats, poultry, and seafoods. Unlike the Eastern school, very few seasonings are used to ensure the preservation of natural vibrant colors and fresh flavors of the food.

The Eastern School — Shanghai

Shanghai has a temperate climate and fertile soil which provides a multitude of crops, such as rice, tea, vegetables, and bamboo shoots. The intricate network of rivers, canals, and lakes springing from the Yangtze provides an abundance of freshwater fish and shellfish, which naturally plays a prominent role in the cuisine.

Shanghai is often considered to be the culinary center for many of the eastern provinces. Among the more well-known seafood delicacies are crab, prawns, and carp. But one can find just about any type of seafood dish prepared by the chefs of Shanghai, along with meats and poultry. Dishes from this region tend to be richer, heavier, and more highly seasoned with salt and sugar. Red-cooked dishes, or cooking foods with soy sauce over low heat, are also characteristic of the eastern region of China.

The Western School — Sichuan and Hunan

Sichuan province is located in a relatively isolated area in the heart of China, where the climate is hot and humid. Regional dishes from this area offer an intriguing, often surprising combination of hot, sour, sweet, and salty flavors.

This unique blend of flavors is achieved through the heavy use of aromatic Sichuan peppercorns and hot chilies. However, not all dishes from this area are spicy. Garlic, soy beans, and ginger are also commonly used.

Hunan province is southeast of Sichuan province. The cuisine of these two neighboring regions is often grouped together, although the two regions are quite different topographically. The fertile rolling hills of Hunan province produce a greater abundance of vegetables. Hunan dishes also include a number of marinated and preserved meats. On the whole, Hunan cuisine tends to be richer than Sichuan cuisine.

34

Rice, Noodles, Flours, and Starches

Bean Thread Noodles

Fun Xi; Fen Si
粉絲

Semi-transparent bean thread noodles, made from mung bean starch, look like bunches of stiff nylon fishing line. Also called cellophane noodles or Chinese vermicelli, they come in a number of different lengths and thicknesses depending on their country of origin.

The delicate mild-flavored noodles are perfect in soups and go especially well in casseroles that have thick sauces and rich seasonings. Just soak them in warm water to soften before adding to the dish. Make sure you have enough liquid — these guys soak up a lot. Before deep-frying, separate a bundle of dry bean thread noodles inside a paper bag. Deep-fry the dry noodles a small handful at a time and watch them puff and expand. Use deep-fried bean thread noodles to garnish salads and other dishes.

Bean thread noodles are sold in plastic packages. Store opened packages in a tightly sealed container in a cool, dry place. Bean thread noodles will keep for several months.

Egg Noodles

Seen Darn Min; Hsien Dan Mien
鮮蛋麵

Fresh and dried egg noodles are common throughout China, but are most popular in the Northern region where wheat is grown more abundantly than rice. Like rice, noodles can be eaten any time of the day.

Try eating noodles with savory braised meats and hearty sauces. For an especially healthy treat, toss noodles with lightly seasoned grilled chicken and steamed vegetables. Enjoy them in hearty, hot soups or in cool, lightly dressed salads.

A wide variety of fresh and dried egg noodles are available in plastic packages and cellophane-wrapped boxes. If you visit a noodle shop in Chinatown, you may find dozens of noodles with varying widths, sizes, and flavors. Store fresh noodles in the refrigerator for up to a week or freeze for up to several months. Keep dried egg noodles in a tightly sealed container in a cool, dry place. They will keep for several months.

Egg Roll Wrappers

May Sig Ce Kuen Pay; Mei Shih Chun Chuan Pi
美式春卷皮

Egg roll wrappers are basically made from wheat flour, eggs, and water. The dough is rolled into thin, pliable sheets similar to the color and texture of wonton wrappers. Most Chinese restaurants use the egg roll wrapper to make your favorite crunchy fried Egg Roll. Don't confuse egg roll wrappers with spring roll wrappers which are thinner. Although they are used in similar ways, they are not the same and are not always interchangeable.

Fill egg roll wrappers with anything from savory leftover vegetables to sweet dried fruit and crunchy nuts, then deep-fry until golden brown. Fried wrappers will have a semi-crispy, bubbly outer shell. Serve savory egg rolls with sweet and sour sauce or soy sauce.

Store the wrappers in a self-sealing plastic bag in the refrigerator for up to a week or freeze for up to several months. Defrost frozen wrappers in the bag to retain their moisture. When working with the wrappers, take out only a few at a time and cover the rest with a damp cloth to prevent them from drying.

Glutinous Rice Flour

Nor Mike Fun; Nuo Mi Fen 糯米粉
(Japanese) Komeko 米粉

Glutinous or sweet rice flour or powder is made from ground glutinous rice. It is used most often to create sweet doughs for Chinese dim sum and many other Chinese and Japanese pastries. When the dough is boiled it forms a smooth, chewy casing. Deep-frying the dough yields a lightly crisp, golden brown outside with a sweet tasting, sticky inside. Japanese mochiko is similar to glutinous rice flour but it is made from ground cooked glutinous rice. Don't confuse these flours with rice flour. Rice flour is made from ground long-grain rice and is used to make rice paper, rice noodles, steamed cakes, and other dim sum dishes.

Deep-fried doughs are filled with spiced stir-fried meats or sweet fillings such as lotus seed or sweet red bean pastes. Steamed doughs traditionally surround sweet black sesame paste, ground peanuts, or shredded coconut fillings.

Glutinous rice flour and rice flour are available in small boxes and packages. Store flours separately in tightly sealed containers in a cool, dry place for up to several months.

Rice, Long-Grain

Jim Mike; Chan Mi
粘米

Rice is one of the most basic foods in Asia, common to nearly all Asian cuisines. Long-grain rice is the everyday rice preferred by most Chinese. Of all the rice varieties, long-grain rice is the least starchy. Because of this characteristic, long-grain rice cooks up dry and fluffy and has grains that separate easily. This makes long-grain rice the perfect candidate for fried rice recipes.

There are several aromatic long-grain rice varieties that are now commonly available in the United States. Highly aromatic Basmati rice is very popular in India and the Middle East. Floral scented Jasmine rice is grown in Thailand.

Long-grain rice is available in various sized plastic bags and woven sacks. Store uncooked rice in a tightly sealed container in a cool, dry place for up to several months. Store cooled cooked rice in the refrigerator for up to several days. It can be easily reheated in a steamer or microwave oven.

Rice, Medium-Grain

Tzoan Mike; Chung Mi
中米

Medium-grain rice is shorter than long-grain rice. It is a popular favorite in eastern areas of China, Taiwan, and of course in Japan and Korea where it is eaten as a daily staple. It is medium-grain rice which appears in Japanese sushi. It is cooked in the same manner as long-grain rice but with slightly less water. When cooked, medium-grain rice is shinier, stickier, and nuttier in texture. To make the rice less sticky, use a little less water to cook.

In regards to all varieties of rice, it is sometimes necessary to rinse and drain the rice several times before adding the final cooking water. Check the package directions first, as some brands enrich the rice with vitamins and minerals which should not be rinsed away.

Medium grain rice is available in various sized plastic bags and woven sacks. Store uncooked rice in a tightly sealed container in a cool, dry place. It will keep for several months. Place cooled cooked rice in a tightly sealed container and store in the refrigerator for up to several days. It can be easily reheated in a steamer or microwave oven.

Rice, Glutinous

Nor Mike; Nuo Mi
糯米

Glutinous rice is a variety of short-grain rice. In its uncooked form, glutinous rice resembles an opaque white, rice-shaped pearl. When cooked it becomes soft, moist, sweet, sticky, and translucent. It is commonly used in Chinese, Japanese, and many South-east Asian cuisines.

Also known as sweet or sticky rice, glutinous rice is a popular ingredient in Chinese lotus wraps and rice puddings. During the Chinese Dragon Boat Festival, glutinous rice is found wrapped in bamboo leaves with salted duck eggs, roast pork, and a treasure of other savory goodies. The Japanese pound cooked glutinous rice to a paste and combine it with sweet fillings to make New Year's mochi cakes. Thai and other Southeast Asian cooks combine glutinous rice with coconut milk and palm sugar to make sweet puddings.

Glutinous rice is usually steamed rather than boiled. Many cooks prefer soaking the grains in water for several hours to overnight before steaming or boiling.

Rice Crusts

Farn Tziu; Fan Chiao
飯焦

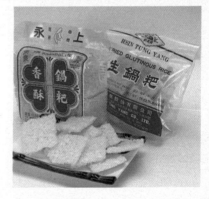

Rice crusts are thin, hard 1½-inch wafers of dried cooked long or medium-grain rice. Rice crusts, also known as rice cakes, are deep-fried to yield puffy-light, slightly crunchy squares which are about three times their original size. They have a taste and texture similar to American rice cake snacks.

For Sizzling Rice Soup, deep-fry the rice crusts and immediately add to soup just before serving to create a sizzling sensation. Rice crusts also make a wonderful base for stir-fried dishes. Just pour the hot stir-fry over a platter of fried rice crusts.

Rice crusts are available in packages of 15 to 20 crusts per bag. Store an opened package in a tightly sealed container in a cool, dry place. It will keep for several months.

Rice Noodles, Fresh

Seen Hor Fun (Chow Hor Fun); Hsien Ho Fen (Chao Ho Fen) 鮮河粉 (炒河粉) (Vietnamese) **Bánh Phở, Tươi**

Fresh rice noodles are made from long-grain rice flour. They are soft, pliable, milky white noodles which can be found in whole folded sheets, wide cut strips, or as thin spaghetti-like strands in the refrigerated section of Asian markets. A light coating of oil prevents them from sticking to each other.

Fresh rice noodles are best stir-fried which yields a crispy edged, soft-centered, gelatinous noodle. A popular restaurant favorite is Chinese Beef Chow Fun with Black Bean Sauce. Add rice noodles to soups or serve with saucy stir-fried dishes in place of rice.

Fresh rice noodles are available packaged in plastic bags or in plastic-wrapped foam trays. Choose those that are soft and spongy to the touch. Although fresh rice noodles are best the day of purchase, they can be stored in the refrigerator for up to several days. The noodles will be stiff after refrigeration, so rinse them gently with boiling water before cooking. This will soften the noodles and remove the oily coating.

Rice Noodles, Dried

Gon Hor Fun; Kan Ho Fen 乾河粉 (Thai) Senlek **เส้นก๋วยเตี๋ยว**

Like fresh rice noodles, dried rice noodles are made from long-grain rice flour. Compared to fresh rice noodles, soaked dried rice noodles are firmer and more brittle in texture. Dried rice noodles are used in light soups, clay pots, and tossed noodle dishes like Pad Thai.

Before stir-frying or using in soups, soak dried rice noodles in water to soften. Gently untangle the noodles before draining. Thin dried rice noodles, called rice sticks, can be deep-fried. Separate dry rice sticks inside a paper-bag and deep-fry a handful at a time. Use the crunchy white noodles as a garnish around stir-fried dishes or toss into salads.

There are many types of dried noodles with varying widths and lengths available in plastic packages. Store an opened package of noodles in a tightly sealed container in a cool, dry place. It will keep for several months.

Rice Papers

Mike Tzee; Mi Chih 米纸
(Vietnamese) **Bánh Tráng**

These brittle, semi-transparent, round or triangular sheets are either called rice papers or rice sheets. The thin, dry sheets made from rice flour can be distinguished by the unique cross-hatch pattern which forms while sun-drying on bamboo mats. Rice papers are used in many Southeast Asian countries but are most common in Vietnamese cuisine. They are similar in size to Mexican tortillas and are used similarly to wrap up savory bundles of meat and dressed vegetables, after which they can be deep-fried or eaten fresh without further cooking.

Soften rice papers between the folds of a dampened tea towel or use a pastry brush to lightly coat them with water before using. Make sure the rice paper edges do not overlap, otherwise they will stick to each other and become unmanageable. In a minute or two they will soften and be ready to use.

Store rice papers flat in a plastic bag in a cool, dry place for up to several months.

Spring Roll Wrappers

Ce Kuen Pay; Chun Chuan Pi
春卷皮

Spring roll wrappers are simply made of wheat flour and water. The thin batter is poured and steamed to form a paper thin pancake. Don't confuse these wrappers with egg roll wrappers which are used to make the Chinese-American favorite Egg Roll. When deep-fried, spring roll wrappers become crisp and smooth with a light-texture. Although spring roll wrappers and egg roll wrappers are used in similar ways, they are not the same and are not always interchangeable.

Fill wrappers with leftover vegetables and meats and deep-fry. Serve with a variety of different dipping sauces, such as soy sauce, Chinese hot mustard, or Worcestershire sauce.

Square and round spring roll wrappers are available in plastic packages. Store the wrappers in a tightly sealed plastic bag in the refrigerator for up to a week or freeze for up to several months. Defrost frozen wrappers in the bag to retain their moisture. When working with the wrappers, take out only a few at a time and cover the rest with a damp cloth to prevent them from drying.

Tapioca Starch

Sike Mike; Hsi Mi
西米

Tapioca starch comes from the root of the cassava plant. It is often used in combination with rice flour or wheat starch to add strength to dim sum doughs. As with cornstarch, tapioca starch is a fine, waxy-textured, white powder typically used for thickening sauces. Some Chinese chefs prefer using tapioca starch to cornstarch because it takes less tapioca starch to thicken sauces and because it is more stable upon reheating.

Tapioca starch, also labeled as tapioca flour or powder, is further processed to make an assortment of granular forms which range from the size of a mustard seed to the size of a green pea. Granular forms of tapioca starch are called tapioca pearls and are used to thicken sauces and make creamy puddings and sweet desserts.

Tapioca starch and tapioca pearls are available in boxes and plastic packages. Store an opened package of tapioca in a tightly sealed container in a cool, dry place. Tapioca starch will keep for several months.

Wheat Starch

Dung Min; Teng Mien
澄麵

Wheat starch is wheat flour with all the gluten removed. It is a fine textured, off-white powder which is commonly used to make doughs in various dim sum dishes. When wheat starch dough is steamed, it becomes soft, shiny, and opaque white. Incorporated into batters, it makes light, airy cakes.

Fill wheat starch doughs with shrimp, minced meat, or fresh vegetable mixtures and pinch to seal. Deep-fry, boil, or steam the dumplings for snacks or appetizers.

Wheat starch is available in cellophane-wrapped packages. Store the contents of an opened package in a tightly sealed container in a cool, dry place. It will keep for several months.

Wonton Wrappers

Won Ton Pay; Yun Tun Pi
雲吞皮

Wonton wrappers are made from wheat flour, water, and eggs. With simple or fancy folds, these 3½-inch squares become delicate envelopes which hold a variety of fillings ranging from savory meats to sweet preserves.

Wrappers are available in different thicknesses and shapes including round wrappers used to make siu mai and potstickers. The cooking technique determines the thickness of the wrapper to use. Basically, thick wrappers are used for deep-frying, pan-frying, and steaming, and thin wrappers are used in soups.

Wonton wrappers are available in plastic packages. Round wrappers may be a bit harder to find. Use a round cookie cutter or scissor to cut out a circle from a square wrapper if necessary. Store wrappers in the refrigerator for up to a week or freeze for up to several months. Defrost frozen wrappers in the bag to retain their moisture. When working with the wrappers, take out only a few at a time and cover the rest with a damp cloth to prevent them from drying.

Growing Your Own Vegetables

Many varieties of fresh Asian vegetables are available throughout the year in local supermarkets. Asian markets carry an even greater supply of fresh as well as many preserved vegetables. The latter of which are enjoyed for their unusual texture and flavor qualities. If you cannot find your favorite Asian vegetables in the supermarket, why not try growing your own? It's fun and easy.

Asian vegetables can be divided into two categories: cool-weather and warm-weather. Generally, leafy green vegetables such as bok choy and cilantro, as well as vegetables which mature underground such as Chinese turnips, grow well during the cooler months of early spring (or fall in mild-winter areas). Chinese broccoli and snow peas also grow well during these months.

Later in the spring, plant warm-season gourds and squashes, such as winter melon, yard long beans, and Chinese okra, to mature in the summer and fall. Consult your local nursery for appropriate planting dates for both cool and warm-weather crops.

A variety of vegetables seeds are available in Asian markets and some nurseries. They are also available by mail from the following seed companies:

Kitazawa Seed Company
1111 Chapman Street
San Jose, CA 95126
(408) 243-1330

Vermont Bean Seed Company
Garden Lane
Fair Haven, VT 07543
(802) 273-3400

Fruits and Vegetables

Fresh
Produce

Asian Pear

Ah Tzou Suet Lay; Ya Chou Hsueh Li
亞洲雪梨

Juicy like a pear, crisp like an apple, Asian pears, also called apple pears, are the oldest cultivated pears known. They have the squatty look of an apple, a sandy texture, and a speckled yellow green or light brown skin of a pear. Generally they are blander in flavor than European pears.

Most people prefer peeling the edible skin of the Asian pear before eating the fruit. Cut it into wedges, matchstick pieces, or dice and eat as is or in mixed salads and desserts. No matter how you prepare the fruit, it will make a refreshing treat any time of the day.

Asian pears are available from summer through fall. Rather than being stacked as most apples and pears are, Asian pears are nestled in foam nets to prevent the delicate fruits from bruising. Choose firm, fragrant Asian pears. Unlike most other pears, Asian pears are ripe even when they do not yield to pressure. Store at room temperature for up to a week or refrigerate for up to a month.

Asian Eggplant

Aike Gwa; Chieh Tzi 矮瓜   茄子
(Japanese) Nasubi なすび

There are several popular Asian eggplants, including the Chinese, Japanese, and Thai varieties. Chinese and Japanese eggplants range in size from short and pudgy 3 inches to thin and slender 9 inches in length. Chinese eggplants are white to lavender; Japanese varieties are light purple to purple-black. Thai eggplants come as small as peas to as large as golf balls. Their skin color ranges from white to lime green with some striped and others solid. Under the skin, however, most varieties are pretty much alike, and with the exception of Thai eggplants, can be used interchangeably in most recipes.

Because Asian eggplants are sweet and relatively seedless, they do not need to be salted, soaked, or peeled. Cut them in half lengthwise or fan cut to grill; for stir-fried or braised dishes, they can be roll cut, sliced, or cubed. Thai eggplants are used cooked in curries; they are used uncooked in chili sauces or pickled.

Choose firm, smooth, unblemished Asian eggplants. They are best when used the day of purchase but can be wrapped in plastic wrap and refrigerated for up to several days.

Bean Sprouts

Look Dou Ah; Lu Tou Ya 芽菜
(Japanese) Moyashi もやし

Fresh bean sprouts, both mung and soy, have bright silver white bodies with yellow heads and long tails. Soy bean sprouts have larger heads and are more crunchy. Fancy restaurants typically remove the head and root portion from the sprouts before cooking to give dishes a clean look, but both the head and root are completely edible and are quite nutritious.

Asians prefer eating bean sprouts stir-fried or boiled with very little seasoning. Try tossing bean sprouts in noodle dishes and fresh salads. Just rinse them with water to clean and remove any unwanted woody green seed hulls before using.

Choose dry, firm, unbroken white bean sprouts. Mung bean sprouts are available in all supermarkets but soy bean sprouts may be a bit harder to find. Sprouts are best used the same day of purchase but they can be refrigerated in a plastic bag with its end opened for up to a couple of days.

Bok Choy

Bok Choy; Pai Tsai
白菜

Bok choy is a loose-leafed cabbage with thick white stalks and dark green leaves. The 7 to 9 inch stalks are mildly tangy and crunchy; leaves are peppery and soft. Baby bok choy is a smaller, younger version of bok choy. Shanghai baby bok choy is another variety which is jade green with spoon-shaped stalks and curved leaves. Both baby and Shanghai bok choy are sweeter and less fibrous than regular bok choy.

All types of bok choy are delicious when lightly stir-fried or boiled. Trim the stem end and diagonally slice the large stalks. Leave baby versions whole, or cut in half or quarter. Serve with light sauces that accent the vegetable's natural sweetness.

Choose bok choy with firm stalks, bright color, and no blemishes. Baby and Shanghai bok choy are sold individually or in small bunches. Refrigerate all types for up to a week.

Chili Peppers

(Fresh) Seen Laut Tziu; Hsien La Chiao
(Dried) Laut Tziu Gon; La Chiao Kan
鮮辣椒　　辣椒乾

Dozens of chilies, both fresh and dried, are
an important flavoring agent in many
regions of China and in most Southeast
Asian countries. Red or green, use whatever
variety you like. In general, the smaller the
chili, the hotter it is. The tiny 1½-inch Thai
bird chili is one of the hottest available. The
slightly larger serrano is just a bit milder, followed by the broad shouldered jalapeño and
the 5-inch Anaheim which still has a gentle kick.

Whole dried red chilies are small, deep red, and fiery hot. Use whole or break into smaller
pieces. Crushed red pepper flakes, which are chopped whole dried red chilies, are a bit hotter
since the seeds and veins are exposed. Buy whole and crushed chilies that are bright red.
Remember to wash your hands after handling any chili; their oils may burn or irritate your skin.

Store fresh chilies in a paper bag and refrigerate for up to two weeks. Store opened packages of
dried chilies in a tightly sealed container in a cool, dry place. They will keep for several months.

Chinese Broccoli

Gai Lan; Chieh Lan
芥蘭

Chinese broccoli doesn't look anything like
the regular broccoli found in most supermarkets. It has thin, dusty green stems,
deep green leaves, and tiny white flowers.
When cooked, the tender stems and leaves
have a slight bitter-sweet taste.

Steamed Chinese broccoli seasoned with
oyster-flavored sauce is a popular Chinese
favorite. Unlike regular broccoli, Chinese
broccoli stems are usually tender and do not need to be peeled, however, if the stems are
thick and appear tough, peel the outer layer before cooking. When stir-frying or boiling,
cook the stems first, then add the more delicate leaves.

Choose young Chinese broccoli with slender stems and unblemished leaves. Thick stems
are a sign of age and may be fibrous and bitter tasting. Refrigerate Chinese broccoli for
up to a week.

Chinese Chives

Gou Choy; Chiu Tsai
韭菜

There are several varieties of Chinese chives used in Asian cooking. Green chives look like wide, 9-inch blades of grass. Yellow chives have shorter, less fibrous leaves and a mild onion-garlic flavor and aroma. Flowering chives are 11 to 12 inches in length and have firm stalks with small edible flower buds at the tips.

Cut Chinese chives into 1½-inch pieces and add to any dish. Try combining yellow chives with tossed noodle dishes, flowering chives with marinated beef to make a tasty stir-fry, and minced green chives in steamed dim sum.

Chinese chives are available in bunches only during the spring and summer seasons. To store, wrap the chives with a damp paper towel, place them in a plastic bag, and refrigerate. The chives will keep for several days; their flavor becomes stronger over time.

Chinese Okra

See Gwa; Ssu Kua
絲瓜

You can't miss Chinese okra. It is the funny looking vegetable with long, bumpy ridges that flow from top to bottom. It has a dull green color and a spongy zucchini-like inner texture. The taste and texture is similar to common okra, but without the thickening qualities.

Before using Chinese okra, peel the bitter, bumpy ridges, then thinly slice or roll cut. Add to stir-fries, soups, or braised dishes.

Choose small Chinese okra, as larger ones tend to be older and more fibrous. They should be firm and unblemished. Refrigerate Chinese okra for up to a week.

Chinese and Japanese Turnips

Law Bok; Lo Po 蘿卜
(Japanese) Kabu かぶ

Chinese and Japanese turnips look like
over-sized carrots. They range in size from
8 to 14 inches long, 2 to 3 inches wide, and
have a grayish white color. The Japanese
variety is also known as daikon or giant
white radish. Although there are many varieties, they all taste sweet and peppery.

The white turnip is a staple in Chinese,
Japanese, and Korean cooking. Among
other uses, Japanese cooks finely shred the
turnip and serve it in salads or as an accompaniment to sashimi. Chinese cooks cut it
into small chunks and add it to stews. Korean cooks pickle the turnip to make kimchee
and other side dishes. Chinese and Japanese turnips can be peeled before cooking, as the
skin can be bitter and tough.

Choose a turnip that is short with a firm, smooth surface. Longer turnips tend to be
older and more fibrous. To prevent moisture loss, wrap the turnip in plastic wrap and
refrigerate. It will keep for a couple of weeks.

Cilantro

Yim Sike; Yuan Chien 芫茜
(Thai) Pak Chi ผักชี

Cilantro, also known as fresh coriander or
Chinese parsley, is one of the most common fresh herbs used in Asian cooking. It is
delightfully aromatic and has a distinct,
refreshing flavor. Don't confuse cilantro
with Italian parsley. Cilantro is the one with
wide, flat leaves.

The Chinese use cilantro as a garnish and to
flavor soups, salads, dim sum stuffings, and
steamed fish. Thai cooks crush cilantro roots
and stems into curry pastes and chili sauces and use the leaves in salads. If you find
cilantro with its roots intact, use the leaves, stems, and roots for a more concentrated flavor.

Choose bright, perky bunches of cilantro with fresh crisp leaves and stems. To store,
stand cilantro in a glass of water, loosely cover the tops with a plastic bag, and refrigerate
for up to several days.

Ginger

Geung; Chiang 薑
(Japanese) Shouga しょうが

In Chinese and Japanese cooking, there is no substitute for fresh ginger. Its spicy bite and tantalizing aroma enhance almost every kind of dish. Ginger looks like a knobby hand with shiny, smooth, golden skin and a fibrous, yellow-green interior. Young ginger or baby ginger is immature when harvested and has a smoother, more delicate flavor and a less fibrous texture.

For aesthetic reasons, many cooks peel ginger before using, although it is not necessary. Thin-skinned young ginger does not need to be peeled. Slice, julienne, mince, or grate ginger and use it to season meats, poultry, seafood, and vegetables dishes.

Choose ginger that is hard, heavy, and free of wrinkles and mold. Ginger is available all year round, but young ginger is available only during the summer and fall seasons. Store mature ginger in a cool, dry place for up to a couple of weeks or peel, place in a jar of dry sherry, and refrigerate for up to several months. Refrigerate young ginger for up to a week.

Jicama

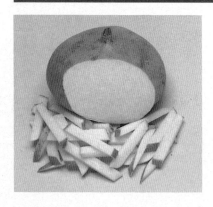

Sa Gog; Sha Chiao
沙角

Jicama looks like the world's largest turnip, with a tan, leathery skin and crunchy, slightly sweet, white flesh. This root vegetable is quite unique for its ability to retain a refreshing crisp texture even after cooking. Although a bit more fibrous and not as sweet tasting, it is a good substitute for fresh water chestnuts.

Jicama may be eaten raw or cooked, but it must be peeled first. Use a sharp paring knife to remove the tough skin. Cut the flesh into matchstick pieces or small chunks and use in salads, stews, and stir-fried dishes.

Choose small, firm, well-rounded jicama that are free of blemishes and mold. Some supermarkets sell quartered or halved jicama wrapped in plastic — a real convenience if you don't need a large piece. Refrigerate uncut pieces for up to several weeks. Wrap cut jicama in plastic wrap and refrigerate for up to a week.

Kumquat

Gum Quat; Kan Chu
柑橘

You probably have seen kumquats in the supermarket and didn't even know what they were. They come in a variety of colors, shapes, and sizes from bright orange to golden yellow, round to oval, and 1 to 1½ inches in length. The kumquat is completely edible with most varieties having a sweet peel and sweet-tart pulp. Some of the Japanese varieties have a sour tasting flesh.

Garnish a platter with whole or sliced kumquats or use them to top sweet desserts. Use the kumquat peel as you would orange and lemon peels. Kumquats are also available preserved in syrup and candied. These sweet treats, found during the Chinese New Year, symbolize good fortune.

Kumquats are seasonal and are available only from October through May. Choose those that are firm with a smooth, shiny, even color. They are best when fresh, but they can be refrigerated for up to a couple of weeks.

Mushrooms

Seen Gu; Hsien Ku 鮮菇
(Japanese) Nama-Shiitake 生椎茸

Mushrooms have long been considered a delicacy in Asian cuisines. There are several types of mushrooms that are especially popular: the delicate, shell-shaped oyster mushroom, the long-stemmed, tiny-capped enoki mushroom, and the firm, golden brown shiitake mushroom. Oyster mushrooms and enoki mushrooms have a mild, delicate flavor; shiitake mushrooms have a rich, meaty flavor. All are smooth and velvety in texture.

Before using the mushrooms, trim off the knobby, woody stem ends. Stir-fry whole oyster or shiitake mushrooms with vegetables or thinly slice and saute. Garnish light soups and fresh salads with a small bunch of enoki mushrooms.

Most mushrooms are available in plastic packages and in bulk. Choose mushrooms that are firm, dry, plump, and free of blemishes. They are best used the day of purchase but will keep for several days if removed from their packages, placed in a paper bag, and refrigerated.

Napa Cabbage

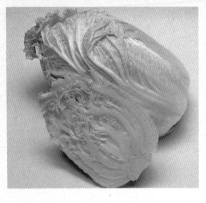

Siu Choy; Shao Tsai 紹菜（天津大白菜）
(Japanese) Hakusai 白菜

Two types of napa cabbage are commonly available: the short, football-shaped Chinese napa cabbage, and the tall, bouquet-shaped Japanese napa cabbage. Both have sweet, creamy white stalks with frayed, ruffled, pale green edges.

Napa cabbage, also called celery cabbage, can be used in the same way as regular cabbage, but because it is more tender, you need to decrease the cooking time. Cut the stalks into small pieces and stir-fry until crisp-tender. Add thinly sliced napa cabbage to soups and cook until translucent and silky textured.

Although the Chinese and Japanese napa cabbages are seasonal, one of the two is likely to be available throughout the year. Choose cabbages with moist, pale green leaves with no browned edges. Ignore the black spots found on the base as they are the result of unpredictable growing conditions. Both varieties of napa cabbage will keep in the refrigerator for a couple of weeks.

Pomelo

Sa Tin You; Sha Tien You
沙田柚

If you've seen a very large, pear-shaped, yellow grapefruit, then you've seen a pomelo, also known as Chinese grapefruit. It has a thick, fragrant peel, and a sweet, dry pulp that is much different from other citrus fruits. The thick membrane surrounding the pulp is inedible and must be removed.

To eat a pomelo, remove the thick peel and membrane and pull apart the sweet pulpy sections. Eat it out of hand or add it to crunchy salads. Dry the peel and use it in soups to add a light citrus fragrance. During the Chinese New Year, you may see pomelos in window displays as they symbolize continued good fortune and prosperity.

Pomelos are available from January through March. Choose fruits that are fragrant and heavy. Refrigerate ripe pomelos for up to a week; let the unripe ones sit on the counter until slightly softened.

Snow Peas

Hor Lan Dou; Hsueh Tou
荷蘭豆 雪豆

Snow peas are flat pea pods with a sweet sugary flavor and crisp, crunchy texture. Unlike English peas which must be shelled before cooking, bright green snow peas are completely edible. They are excellent in stir-fries, salads, and soups.

To use, snap off the stem ends and remove the fibrous strings that run along the sides. Boil, steam, or stir-fry until crisp-tender, and add to any dish that needs green accents or texture. To make snow peas more decorative, cut them in half diagonally or cut out a tiny triangle from the stem ends.

Be sure to pick young snow peas which are bright green, flat, crisp, and free of blemishes. Avoid wilted, thick-skinned, overly plump, and discolored peas as they are too mature and more fibrous. Snow peas will keep in the refrigerator for a week. Frozen snow peas are available but are not recommended.

Taro Root

Woo Tou; Yu Tou
芋頭

There are many types and sizes of taro root including the large melon-sized taro and the small golf ball-sized taro. All are somewhat hairy, dark-skinned, and rough textured on the outside. The flesh of some varieties turns from white or grayish to light purple when cooked. Starchy in texture, cooked taro root is sweet and nutty in flavor.

Before using, taro root must be peeled and cooked to become edible. Wear rubber gloves when peeling taro root, as the juices may irritate your skin. Use the root as you would use potatoes. Shred taro root and deep-fry to make an edible basket. Boil or steam taro root and blend into stuffings. Cut it into chunks and add to stews and braised dishes. As with potatoes, taro root goes well with rich seasonings and sauces.

Look for firm taro roots that are free of dents, wrinkles, blemishes, and mold. Store taro roots in a cool, dry place. They will keep for a week.

Winter Melon

Doan Gwa; Tung Kua
冬瓜

If you ever saw a winter melon, you might have thought it was a dusty, old green pumpkin. It is a pretty interesting looking vegetable with the entire surface covered with chalky white bloom. Inside is a tangled web of seeds which must be removed before cooking. The inner flesh is pale green to milky white in color with a faint sweet-peppery taste.

Winter melon is never eaten raw. Remove the seeds and rind, thinly slice, and steam or simmer in soups. Because it has a relatively bland flavor, winter melon is typically paired with flavorful ingredients, such as dried shrimp and dried black mushrooms in soups and stir-fried dishes.

Winter melons can weigh from 8 to 10 pounds and be 12 to 15 inches tall. Because of their huge size, most Asian markets cut them before selling them to their customers. Store an uncut melon in a cool, dry place for up to a month. Wrap cut melon in plastic wrap and refrigerate for up to several days.

Yard Long Beans

Dou Gog; Tou Chiao
豆角

The yard long bean isn't one yard long, but it can grow to a length of 18 inches. It's sort of like the story about the fish that got away. They are pencil-thin beans with smooth, somewhat bumpy surfaces. Their color ranges from pale green to dark green. When cooked, long beans have a sweet flavor and a dry, crunchy bite unlike other string beans which are juicy and crisp.

Trim the stem ends of the beans before cooking — notice there's no fibrous strings to remove. Cut long beans into ½-inch, 1-inch, or 2-inch pieces and stir-fry. For a fancier presentation, cut long beans into 6 to 8 inch lengths, blanch until softened, and tie each into a knot. Serve the long bean knots as a side dish with roasted meats and poultry.

Yard long beans are found tied in bunches. Although they are available all year around, they are at their best during the summer season. Buy young beans which have few blemishes and wrinkles. Older beans, which tend to be longer, are tough and fibrous. Yard long beans will keep in the refrigerator for a week.

A Dim Sum Experience

Dim sum literally means point (dim) to the heart (sum) or "touches the heart," and after eating these tasty morsels, you'll agree that they were appropriately named. The dozens of savory dumplings, sweet-filled pastries, and steamed breads are commonly eaten as a light breakfast, snack, or lunch in Chinese restaurants and tea houses — places where family, friends, and business associates gather to eat throughout North America and other parts of the world.

If you have never experienced the pleasures of dim sum, you might want to go with someone who is familiar with the selections. There aren't always menus in Chinese tea houses. To order, you must get the attention of passing waitresses pushing carts stacked high with tiny steamers and hot food trays, each holding a different treat. Just point to a dish and it's yours. Choose as many dishes as you wish, but don't order too many of the same dish. More carts carrying dozens of other delicacies are guaranteed to emerge from the kitchen, and you can bet you will want to try a dish from every passing cart. At the end of the meal, your bill is calculated by the number of empty dishes on the table or by the number of stamps on your bill.

The preparation of dim sum is time consuming, requiring a lot of manpower and skill. Hand-made doughs of wheat starch, rice flour, and wheat flour are rolled out into flat pancakes and are stuffed with countless combinations of meat, vegetables, and sweet bean pastes. Fillings are enclosed by careful folding and pleating of the dough and are then shaped into balls, half-moon crescents, or baskets. The dumplings are then steamed, braised, deep-fried, or baked into mouth-watering morsels bursting with flavor.

Here's a list of some of the more popular items found in Chinese tea houses:

Steamed Items	Pronunciation	Character
Shrimp Dumpling	Har Gau	蝦餃
Pork Dumpling	Siu Mai	燒賣
Chiu Chow Dumpling	Chiu Chow Fun Guor	潮洲粉果
Cilantro Dumpling	Heung Sai Gau	香茜餃
Chinese Chive Dumpling	Gow Choy Gau	韭菜餃
Barbecued Pork Bun	Char Siu Bao	叉燒包
Rice Noodle Roll	Churn Fun	腸粉

Deep-Fried Items:		
Spring Roll	Chun Guen	春卷
Shrimp Toast	Har Dor See	蝦多士
Taro Dumpling	Woo Gok	芋角
Sweet Rice Dumpling	Hom Soi Gok	咸水角

Sweet And Other Savory Selections		
Black Sesame Roll	Gee Mar Guen	芝麻卷
Sesame Seed Ball	Jin Dui Jai	煎堆
Custard Tart	Don Tot	蛋撻
Beef Chow Fun	See Jup Ngau Hor	豉汁牛河

Canned and Preserved Ingredients

Baby Corn

Siu Gum Soeun; Hsiao Chin Sun
小金笋

What is there to say about baby corn,
except that it looks exactly like miniature
ears of corn. Don't just eat the tiny kernels
off the cob; the whole ear is edible with a
sweet taste and crunchy texture. Baby corn,
which may also be labeled as young corn, is
typically 2 to 3 inches in length and mellow
yellow in color.

Before using canned baby corn, drain and
rinse under water to remove any trace of the
salty canning liquid. If baby corn has a metallic taste, blanch the ears in boiling water. Baby
corn is most popular in stir-fried dishes, but can also be used in soups and salads.

Transfer the contents of an opened can of baby corn to a tightly sealed container, fill it with
water, and refrigerate. The baby corn will keep for a week if the water is changed daily.

Bamboo Shoots

Tzook Soeun; Chu Sun
竹笋

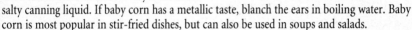

Bamboo shoots come in several varieties
including whole tips, young tips, sliced, or
diced shoots. They all basically have a sweet
taste but their texture varies due to the
amount of fiber present in each cut. Young
winter bamboo tips are most tender, and
sliced shoots are most fibrous.

As with many canned products, bamboo
shoots may have a slight tinny or metallic
taste. To eliminate any off flavors, rinse
them under water or blanch them in boiling water. Bamboo shoots are often combined
with black fungus and vegetables to make wonderful vegetarian dishes. Add crunchy
bamboo shoots to salads, light soups, and savory dim sum fillings.

Asian markets carry the widest selection of bamboo shoots, but small cans of whole and
sliced shoots are available in many supermarkets. Transfer the contents of an opened can
to a tightly sealed container, fill it with water, and refrigerate. The bamboo shoots will
keep for a week if the water is changed daily.

Black Fungus

Hok Mook Yee; Hei Mu Erh
黑木耳

Dried black fungus is the all encompassing name which includes cloud ear, wood ear, tree ear, and a variety of other fungus. Cloud ears are so named because of their resemblance to clouds. Wood and tree ears are grown on wood pieces and old tree stumps, hence their clever name. In their dried form, all look like old leather chips.

Soak dried black fungus in warm water to soften before using and then remove the hard, knobby stem end. Use only a few pieces of fungus at a time — their size will increase threefold with soaking. Cut large ears into bite-size pieces or cut them into thin strips. Black fungus has a crisp bite, a smooth, silky texture, and a bland taste that goes well with any seasoning in stir-fried dishes and soups.

Dried black fungus is available, whole or shredded, in plastic packages. Choose ears that are small and thin rather than large and thick. Store dried black fungus in a tightly sealed container in a cool, dry place. They will keep for several months.

Black Mushrooms, Dried

Gon Doan Gu; Kan Tung Ku 乾冬菇
(Japanese) Kansou-Shiitake 乾燥椎茸

Chinese and Japanese cooks use a variety of dried fungus, and dried black mushrooms are perhaps the most popular. These mushrooms are also known as Chinese black mushrooms. Their Japanese cousins are called dried shiitake mushrooms. They all have brownish-black caps, tan undersides, a rich, meaty texture, and a wild mushroom flavor.

For stir-fried dishes and stuffings, use the less expensive dried black "winter" mushroom. For whole mushroom dishes, use the dried black "flower" mushroom. This mushroom has light tan creases in the cap which resemble a flower. The more expensive Japanese type of flower mushroom has the best texture and richest flavor. Soak all dried black mushrooms in warm water before using, then cut off the hard, knobby stem end. Strain the soaking liquid if you wish and use it to flavor sauces and soups.

Dried black mushrooms are available in plastic packages in Asian markets. Store them in a tightly sealed container in a cool, dry place. They will keep for several months.

Ginger, Preserved

Tong Geung; Tang Chiang
糖薑

Fresh ginger is an important ingredient in everyday Asian cooking, but it is also prepared and used in candied, preserved, and pickled forms. For more information on fresh ginger see page 52.

Pieces of tender young ginger are cooked, then sugar-coated to make delicious candied ginger. Honey-colored candied ginger has an incredible burst of sweet-spicy ginger flavor. Preserved ginger is packed in a heavy sugar syrup which becomes infused with a mild ginger taste. Candied and preserved ginger are delicious chopped and added to ice cream or used to top fresh fruits for dessert. Young pickled ginger is cured in a salt brine, then soaked in a sugar and vinegar solution. Slightly sweeter red pickled ginger is also available.

Candied, preserved, and pickled gingers are available in an assortment of packages, jars, and crocks. Candied ginger will keep for several months in a cool, dry place. Opened jars of preserved and pickled ginger should be refrigerated. They will keep for several months.

Lychee

Like Tzee; Li Chih
荔枝

Fresh lychee looks like a bright, crimson pink berry with a bumpy, leathery skin. With one swift motion the peel is removed revealing the semi-translucent, juicy flesh. With one more swift move it is eaten, leaving behind a single, shiny, smooth, mahogany-colored seed.

Only recently has fresh lychee been available in the United States. Florida growers harvest fresh lychee from July through September. Luckily canned lychees are always available. Both canned and fresh lychee are sugary sweet with a taste and texture similar to soft grapes. Eat lychee slightly chilled as a refreshing snack, served over ice cream, or in colorful fruit salads and sweet and sour dishes.

Pick bunches that are heavy with bright, unblemished skins. Keep them in the refrigerator for up to several weeks. Transfer the contents of an opened can to a tightly sealed container and refrigerate for up to several days.

Sichuan Preserved Vegetables

Tzar Choy; Cha Tsai
榨菜

The name Sichuan preserved vegetables refers to a number of different spicy pickled Chinese vegetables including kohlrabi, mustard greens, napa cabbage, and turnips. Typically covered with a bit of chili powder and ground Sichuan peppercorns, the preserved vegetables are dark olive-green in color with a spicy-salty taste. In traditional Chinese cooking, each vegetable is used in a different way, but for American tastes, all Sichuan preserved vegetables can be used interchangeably in recipes.

Sichuan preserved vegetables come in whole pieces, chunks, slices, and pre-shredded. To cut down on the saltiness, rinse the needed amount of Sichuan preserved vegetable to remove any excess seasoning and pickling brine before using. Cut large pieces into matchstick pieces or finely slice and toss with cold noodles, or finely dice the vegetable and add to meat fillings. Use preserved vegetables any time you want to add a salty crunch to a dish. Sichuan preserved vegetables are found in cans, jars, and loose in large tubs in the refrigerated section of Asian markets. Refrigerate for up to a month.

Straw Mushrooms

Tzo Gu; Tsao Ku
草菇

Straw mushrooms have a delicate sweetness and a firm, meaty texture. The unpeeled variety is preferred by most Chinese chefs. It has a cap which encases the whole body and stem such that it resembles a little brown egg with a slightly flat bottom. The peeled variety is far more interesting looking. It has a brown, domed-shaped cap and a thick, straw-colored stem.

Before using straw mushrooms, drain and rinse under water to remove any trace of the salty canning liquid. If the mushrooms have a metallic taste, blanch them in boiling water. Use either type of straw mushroom in stir-fried meat and vegetable dishes.

Unpeeled straw mushrooms are available in various sized cans and jars. Many supermarkets only carry peeled straw mushrooms. Transfer the contents of an opened can to a tightly sealed container, fill it with water, and refrigerate. It will keep for a week if the water is changed daily.

Water Chestnuts

Ma Tike; Ma Ti
馬蹄

Fresh water chestnuts are squatty, 1½-inch, pointy-topped tubers with a shiny, brown skin. Inside is the sweet, slightly starchy flesh. Canned water chestnuts have a similar texture but they are not as sweet. Both fresh and canned water chestnuts are unique because they retain their crunchy texture long after cooking. Jicama is a good substitute.

Rinse fresh water chestnuts to remove any mud. Peel the brown skin and cut the flesh into thin slices. Place in a bowl of water to prevent discoloration. Rinse canned water chestnuts under water or blanch them in boiling water to eliminate any off flavors.

Fresh water chestnuts may be harder to find, but it is worth the search. Buy those that are free of wrinkles and mold. Store fresh water chestnuts in a paper bag and refrigerate for up to a week, or peel and freeze for up to a month. Transfer the contents of an opened can to a tightly sealed container, fill with water, and refrigerate. The water chestnuts will keep for a week if the water is changed daily.

White Fungus

Suet Yee; Hsueh Erh
雪耳

White fungus resembles a small, hard, round sponge. Its color ranges from golden beige to creamy off-white, which turns silvery-white after cooking. It is prized for its superior crunchy texture which turns slightly gelatinous during cooking. It has little flavor of its own, but readily absorbs the flavors of other ingredients.

White fungus is particularly favored in sweet dessert soups. Soak white fungus in warm water to soften before cooking. Use scissors to remove the hard core from the underside, then cut the fungus into bite-size pieces. Rehydrated white fungus can grow three times its dry size so don't soak too many pieces at one time. Remember, a little goes a long way.

White fungus is available in plastic bags. The better quality and more expensive fungus is packaged in boxes of nine or twelve pieces. Store fungus in a tightly sealed container and keep in a cool, dry place for up to several months.

Other Traditional Ingredients

Agar Agar

Dai Choy Go; Tạ Tsai Kao 大菜糕
(Thai) Woon วุ้น

Agar agar is Asia's answer to unflavored gelatin. It is a seaweed extract that is frequently used to set cold salads and desserts. Because it gels at a higher temperature, agar agar is ideal to use in dishes served at room temperature on even the hottest day.

It is sold in powder, rectangular, and strip forms. Feather-light rectangles are typically brightly colored and 12 to 14 inches long. Strips are 10 to 14 inches long and look like crumpled strands of cellophane tape. Powdered and solid forms of agar agar need to be dissolved in hot water before being used as a jelling agent. Cooking techniques and times vary, so follow packaged directions when using these products. Fine strips of agar agar must be soaked in warm water to soften before using. The strips are most often used to add a crunchy texture to cold tossed salads.

Agar agar is available in plastic packages. Transfer the contents of an opened package to a self-sealing plastic bag and keep in a cool, dry place for up to several months.

Black Vinegar

Hok Tzo; Hei Tsu
黑醋

Bold flavored black vinegar is made from the fermentation of a mixture of rice, wheat, and millet or sorghum. Compared to common white vinegar, black vinegar is less tart, smokier, sweeter, more flavorful, and of course darker in color.

A popular type of black vinegar produced in Eastern China is called Chinkiang vinegar. A milder, lighter, and smoother version of black vinegar is red vinegar. Use either in braised dishes or as a table condiment for dumplings and hot and sour dishes.

Black and red vinegars are available in various sized bottles. If black or red vinegar are unavailable, substitute balsamic vinegar and decrease the amount of sugar the recipe may call for. Store black and red vinegar in a cool, dry place. Both varieties of vinegar will keep for several months, but will lose flavor and intensity over time.

Chinese New Year Candies

Sun Nin Tong Guor; Hsin Nien Tang Kuo
新年糖果

You'll know it's the Chinese New Year when you visit Chinatown and see windows filled with tiny gold printed red envelopes and bright orange tangerines. If you are invited to a Chinese home during this holiday period, you'll be offered an assortment of traditional Chinese New Year candies.

Decorative lacquer trays are filled with a selection of candied treats including sweet lotus seeds, lotus roots, peanuts, kumquats, water chestnuts, and strips of coconut and winter melon. Buy a few bags of each because after the New Year, they won't be as easy to find.

A selection of candies is available during the Chinese New Year in Asian markets. Fortunately, New Year candies and other sweet treats can be found year round in Asian candy stores. Transfer the contents of an opened bag to a jar with a tight fitting lid. Store the candies in a cool, dry place for up to several months.

Chinese Sausage

Larp Tzoen; La Chang
臘腸

If you walked past a Chinese deli you might have seen slender links of Chinese sausages hanging from a rack in the window. The sausage, ranging from 4 to 6 inches in length, is deep red to brown in color and slightly bumpy in texture.

A majority of Chinese sausages are made from pork, pork fat, duck, or beef. They are simply seasoned with salt, sugar, and rice wine and must be cooked before eating. No matter what variety you buy, all are savory-sweet and delicious.

Chinese deli's sell Chinese sausages in pairs; (approximately four pairs equal a pound) and are held together with colored string. The color of the string represents a different type of sausage. The sausages are also available in vacuum-packed packages. Steam or boil the sausages before serving to remove excess fat, or cut them into thin slices and stir-fry with an assortment of vegetables. Store Chinese sausage in the refrigerator for up to a month or freeze for up to several months.

Duck Eggs

(Thousand Year) Pay Darn; Pi Tan 皮蛋
(Salted) Harm Darn; Hsien Tan 咸蛋

In old China, people did not have refrigeration so they preserved many foods, including eggs. The thousand year old duck egg, also known as the hundred year old duck egg, is coated with a mixture of ash, lime, salt, and tea leaves. The 100-day preservation process solidifies the egg white and changes its color to a dark amber and the yolk's color to a grayish-green. Just peel the ash layer and shell and serve with congee or with pickled ginger as a classic appetizer. Refrigerate these eggs for up to a month.

Another preserved egg is the salted duck egg. It's cured in ash and brine for several months which thins the white, makes the yolk firm and orange-colored, and turns the shell grayish blue. The salted duck egg must be cooked before eating. Try it hard-boiled or mix the raw egg with other ingredients and then boil, steam, or stir-fry. Choose eggs that are unblemished and heavy. Gently shake the egg and listen. If you hear a gentle sloshing sound, you've picked a good egg with a firm yolk. Avoid those that sound runny or those that make no sound at all. Refrigerate salted duck eggs for up to a month.

Lotus Leaves, Dried

Gon Hor Yip; Kan Ho Yeh
乾荷葉

In Chinese cuisine, dried lotus leaves are not actually eaten, but are used as a wrapping for savory stuffings of rice and meat which are steamed. During cooking, the leaf imparts an aromatic, smoky flavor to the food. When a single dried leaf is unfolded, it measures almost 2 feet in diameter. The large leaves make excellent wrappers for popular Chinese dishes like Beggar's Chicken and Rice in a Lotus Leaf.

Directions for preparing dried lotus leaves vary according to the recipe. Generally, the idea is to soak or boil the leaves until they are soft and pliable.

Dried lotus leaves are found wrapped in plastic packages. They will keep for several months in a cool, dry place. Dried lotus leaves are brittle, so don't place heavy objects on top of the stored package.

Lychee, Dried

Like Tzee Gon; Li Chih Kan
荔枝乾

Dried lychee, also known as the lychee nut, neither tastes nor looks like fresh or even canned lychee. The reddish brown-colored shell is brittle and inedible; the brown fruit inside looks somewhat like a dried prune. Dried lychee has a smoky-sweet taste.

Dried lychee is usually eaten as a snack right out of the bag. Just remove the brittle shell and nibble at the flesh surrounding the large seed. Cut the flesh from the seed and add to sweet desserts, just as you would raisins, dates, and prunes.

Dried lychees are available in plastic bags and small boxes. Transfer the contents of an opened bag to a container with a tight fitting lid and store in a cool, dry place. Dried lychee will keep for several months.

Peanut Oil

Fa Seng You; Hua Sheng You
花生油

In Chinese and other Asian cooking, the clear golden oil extract from peanuts is highly prized as a cooking oil. Its fragrant aroma and distinct nutty flavor makes peanut oil the ideal oil for stir-frying and deep-frying.

Peanut oil has a high smoke point compared to other cooking oils. This means peanut oil can be heated to a relatively high temperature without burning or breaking down. It is desirable as a deep-frying oil because it does not readily absorb the flavor of the food being fried, so the oil can usually be used once more after straining.

Choose peanut oil that is hot-pressed from roasted peanuts rather than cold pressed if you want all that the oil has to offer. Peanut oil is available in large-sized jugs and bottles in Asian markets. More expensive cold-pressed peanut oil is available in small bottles in supermarkets and some health food stores. Store peanut oil in a cool, dry place. It will keep for several months.

Sesame Seeds

Tzee Ma; Chih Ma 芝麻
(Japanese) Goma ごま

Both black and white sesame seeds are used to flavor and garnish Chinese, Japanese, and Korean dishes. White sesame seeds, hulled and unhulled, have a sweet, nutty flavor. Black sesame seeds are slightly bitter. Unlike black sesame seeds, white sesame seeds should be toasted before using to intensify their flavor and aromatic fragrance.

Sprinkle a spoonful of toasted white sesame seeds over salads, appetizers, and grilled dishes just before serving to give dishes a unique look and taste. Some Japanese and Korean dishes call for grinding the sesame seeds to a coarse powder before using in recipes.

Buying sesame seeds can be expensive if you purchase them in small jars from supermarkets. Both white and black sesame seeds are available in larger quantities and at much lower prices in Asian markets. Choose bags with few broken or blemished seeds. Store the contents of opened bag in a tightly sealed plastic bag and refrigerate. It will keep for up to several months.

Yin and Yang

For thousands of years the Chinese have followed the Taoist philosophy of cosmic equilibrium — the balanced harmony of all things. One of the simplest forms of this philosophy is the idea of two opposing forces in balance — yin and yang. Yin represents the feminine, cooler, moister, and weaker forces, while yang comprises the masculine, warmer, drier, and stronger forces.

Chinese cooks follow this philosophy by selecting a combination of foods that balance yin and yang to keep the body in equilibrium and maintain good health. Foods are cooked, then classified according to how they affect the body. "Cold" or yin foods such as winter melon, asparagus, and crab meat cleanse, soothe, and moisturize the body. "Hot" or yang foods such as chili peppers, ginger, fried foods, and red meats are thought to increase the pulse rate and perspiration. This removes excess moisture from the body.

Many Chinese believe that when the lips crack or the nose bleeds, the body is too dry, and the system has too much yang force. Yin foods should be eaten to bring the body back into balance. When the weather is humid, people tend to be weak and tired, and the body retains too much moisture. Yang foods are then eaten to bring the yin forces back into equilibrium.

When planning your menu, strive for a balance of color, texture, flavor, and cooking techniques. This too is part of the traditional Chinese concept of contrast and balance.

Shrimp Chips

Ha Pin; Hsia Pian
蝦片

Shrimp chips are available as ready-to-eat snack chips and as uncooked pellets.When cooked, the 3-inch chip looks like a colored styrofoam wafer and has a delicate shrimp flavor. Krupuk, an Indonesian variety of shrimp chip, is extra large reaching lengths of 8 to 10 inches.

Uncooked pellets resemble hard vermicelli wafers. The inedible pellets are usually white but are also available in a variety of light pastel colors which make them pretty garnishes as well as tasty snacks when cooked. To cook, heat enough oil for deep-frying until hot and add a few pellets. After the pellets expand, remove the chips to a paper towel and let drain.

Shrimp chips are available in bags; uncooked pellets are found in plastic bags and boxes. Place cooked chips in a tightly sealed container and keep in a cool, dry place for up to a week. Store uncooked pellets in a cool, dry place. They will keep for several months.

Shrimp, Dried

Gon Ha Mi; Kan Hsia Mi
乾蝦米

Tiny shrimp are preserved in brine, then dried, creating slightly chewy morsels with a pungent taste. Their unique flavor will enhance any vegetable dish, soup, or dim sum filling.

Add dried shrimp directly from the package to simmering soups or stir-fry alone and eat them by the handful as a snack. Soak dried shrimp until softened and add to braised meat and stir-fried vegetable dishes. Usually no more than a few tablespoons are used for a recipe that serves four.

Choose packages that have bright, orange-colored shrimp of uniform size. Avoid packages that contain shrimp that are flaky, spotted, gray, or pale colored, as these are often signs of age and poor flavor. Store dried shrimp in a tightly sealed container in a cool, dry place for up to several months.

Tea, Unfermented Green

Look Tza; Lu Cha 緑茶
(Japanese) Ryokucha 緑茶

Teas are divided into three types: unfermented green, semi-fermented, and fermented black. All three types come from the same species of plant, *Camellia sinensis*, but each varies in its method of processing.

Immediately after removing the leaves from the tea plant, those destined to be used in green teas are steamed to prevent any fermentation. At this point the leaves are soft, tender, and pliable. Next the leaves are alternately rolled and dried to prevent further oxidation. This process yields a twisted, light green-colored leaf.

Green tea produces a pale colored brew with a natural bouquet and a pure, refreshing taste. Its flavor is characteristically mild, but it still has a full body. Popular unfermented teas include Chinese Dragon Well tea and Japanese Brown Rice tea, a green tea blended with roasted brown rice. Occasionally, you might find a few grains of brown rice which have burst during the teas roasting process giving brown rice tea its alias name, popcorn tea. Store unfermented green tea in a tightly sealed container in a cool, dry place for up to several months.

Tea, Semi-Fermented

Wu Loan Tza; Wu Lung Cha 烏龍茶
(Japanese) Uuron-Cha ウーロン茶

Semi-fermented teas are processed similarly to black fermented teas but the duration of the fermentation and oxidation stages are shortened. Because it is semi-fermented, the dark green tea leaves take on characteristics of both fermented black and unfermented green teas.

The compromise between green and black teas makes a tawny-colored brew with a pleasant aroma and full body. A well known semi-fermented tea is Oolong tea which comes from China's Fujian province and Taiwan. This tea is characteristically fermented for a relatively shorter period of time and is dried at a higher temperature in comparison to other processes. Not only is it a favorite among Chinese restaurants, but it is also used as the base for fine Jasmine tea which has a delicate perfume-like taste that is as delicious as it is aromatic. Store semi-fermented tea in a tightly sealed container in a cool, dry place for up to several months.

Tea, Fermented Black

Hung Tza; Hung Cha　紅茶
(Japanese) Koucha　紅茶

Leaves destined to be brewed for black tea
go through an initial evaporation stage
called withering. At this point, the leaves
are spread on racks and allowed to wither
and become flexible. They are then rolled
between gentle crushers which release their
juices. Next, the leaves are spread out and
allowed to ferment and oxidize until the
leaves change to a bright copper color. The
tea leaves then go through a final drying
stage which turns them black before being readied for shipment.

When brewed, the infusion gives a clear copper-red liquid with a full body and a strong
flavor. The best known black tea is Keemun, but other Chinese favorites include Lychee
Black tea and Iron Goddess of Mercy. Some popular tea companies will sort and mix
different varieties of tea to produce a unique blend and flavor.

Ginseng

Sum; Shen

Ginseng is one of Asia's most popular and
prized ingredients known for its medicinal
properties. People are willing to pay big bucks
for ginseng roots from China, Japan, and
Korea. It is said that a dying person will literally get up after drinking ginseng tea or soup
made with the ginseng root. Not only do people claim that it purifies the blood and
strengthens the heart, among a dozen other
things, it also makes a refreshing beverage.

Besides its amazing healing powers, the ginseng root is well-known for its unique form.
The legend tells of a man's wailing voice that could be heard through the forest at night.
When investigating townspeople located the source of the cries, they found a beautiful
ginseng root in the shape of a human being. Because of its unique human-like shape,
many Asians believe that ginseng root is a cure to all that ails people. Believe it or not.
Ginseng is available in whole and cut dried forms and as a powder for teas. Store ginseng
root and tea in separate tightly sealed containers and keep in a cool, dry place for up to
several months.

Selected Asian Specialties

Bean Curd

Dou Fu; Tou Fu 豆腐
(Japanese) Toufu 豆腐

There are three main types of bean curd. All are made from soy beans and water, but each type varies slightly in texture. Soft bean curd is silky smooth and very light in texture. Firm and regular bean curd have dense structures and slightly spongy interiors.

Bean curd tastes bland, but it readily absorbs the flavors of other foods and sauces. It is eaten hot or cold, alone or in combination with an array of foods. Cut soft bean curd into tiny cubes and add to hot soups. Gently crumble regular bean curd and toss into hearty salads. Cut firm bean curd into bite-size pieces and stir-fry with meats and vegetables.

Bean curd is available in plastic containers and cartons in the refrigerated section of most supermarkets. Check the package for its preferred storage method and expiration date. Some Asian markets sell loose bean curd which is usually found in tubs of water. Store the cubes in a tightly sealed container, fill with water, and refrigerate. It will keep for several days if the water is changed daily. Discard any bean curd that develops a strong odor.

Bean Curd Puffs

Dou Fu Pork; Tou Fu Po 豆腐卜
(Japanese) Age-Toufu あげ豆腐

Bean curd puffs are pieces of bean curd that have been deep-fried until lightly crispy and golden brown on the outside. Thin puffs have a slightly dry center, and thick puffs have a spongy center. Both add a meat-like texture to dishes.

Before using bean curd puffs, blanch them in boiling water to eliminate excess oil. Slice thin bean curd puffs into strips and add to soups and noodle dishes. Japanese cooks cut off one edge from thin puffs, gently open, then fill the pouches with a mixture of vinegar seasoned medium-grain rice and toasted sesame seeds. Add thick bean curd puffs to stews, or stuff with a savory shrimp filling and braise.

Packaged bean curd puffs are available in cans and in packages in the refrigerated section of most supermarkets. Check the package for storage information and expiration date. Some Asian markets sell loose puffs in large tubs; these tend to be of better quality than packaged puffs. Store loose puffs in a tightly sealed container and refrigerate for up to a week.

Bean Curd Sheets

Fu Tzook; Fu Chu　腐竹
(Japanese) Yuba　ゆば

Dried bean curd sheets are a by-product of bean curd production. When heated soy bean milk is allowed to stand and cool, a thin film-like layer forms on top. This layer is carefully removed and laid over bamboo mats to dry, forming bean curd sheets. The transparent yellow sheets are quite fragile in their dried form but become chewy and meaty when cooked.

Soak bean curd sheets in warm water or place between damp towels until softened before using. Use whole sheets to wrap meat and vegetable fillings. These rolls can be steamed, pan-fried, deep-fried, or braised. Add broken pieces of bean curd sheets to stews and savory and sweet soups.

Bean curd sheets are available in both frozen and dried forms in an assortment of different shapes and sizes. Store dried bean curd sheets in a tightly sealed container and keep in a cool, dry place. Use both frozen and dried sheets within two months of purchase. Discard if an off odor develops.

Bean Curd Sticks

Tzee Tzook; Chih Chu
支竹

Bean curd sticks are made the same way as bean curd sheets, but instead of laying the sheets flat to dry, the sticks are crinkled and placed over rails. Because they are high in protein and low in calories, bean curd sticks make great meat substitutes in vegetarian dishes.

As with bean curd sheets, bean curd sticks must be softened in warm water before using. Cut softened sticks into 3-inch pieces and add to meat or vegetarian dishes. Bland-tasting bean curd sticks readily absorb the flavors of rich seasonings and savory gravies, making them great choices to use in simmering soups and thick stews.

Store bean curd sticks in a tightly sealed container and keep in a cool, dry place. Use bean curd sticks within two months of purchase. Discard if an off odor develops.

Bonito

Geen Pin; Chien Pien 鰹片
(Japanese) Katsuobushi かつおぶし

Bonito is one of the principal ingredients used to make dashi, the traditional Japanese fish stock. Fresh shavings from whole dried bonito fillets make the best dashi, but these fillets are often hard to find and shaving them is a time-consuming process. Machine-shaved bonito flakes, which are of comparable quality, are easy and convenient to use.

Bonito fillets are boiled, smoked, and dried. This lengthy process produces a rock hard, dark gray "brick" covered with a thin moldy ash layer. The flakes shaved from the fillets are very thin and light salmon-pink in color. Use flakes to flavor stocks and sauces. Garnish vegetables and fried dishes with thin bonito threads.

Bonito flakes are available in boxes and plastic packages. Choose those with light colored flakes that look paper thin. Transfer the contents of an opened package to a tightly sealed container and keep in a cool, dry place. The flakes will keep for several months but will lose flavor over time.

Coconut Milk

Yare Nai; Yeh Nai 椰奶
(Thai) Kathi กะทิ

Most people have seen a round brown coconut, and everyone has tasted shredded sweet coconut in cookies and cakes, but until recently, coconut milk has remained something of a hard-to-find ingredient. There's nothing exotic about a coconut in Southeast Asia; it is used for its water, milk, cream, and shredded meat. For more information on coconuts see page 87.

Coconut milk is used to make dozens of dishes from soups and sauces to curries and desserts. Follow your recipe's instructions for extracting fresh coconut milk, as many chefs have different definitions and methods of removal. If you prefer, use canned coconut milk, a popular option when good-quality fresh coconuts are not available. Generally, if a recipe calls for thick coconut milk or coconut cream, spoon off the thick layer from the top of an unshaken can. The liquid remaining in the bottom of the can is thin coconut milk. If a recipe just calls for coconut milk, shake the can and use the blended contents.

Refrigerate coconut milk for up to several days. Discard if a sour odor develops.

Curry

Ga Lay Jeng; Ka Li Chiang　咖喱醬
(Thai) Nam Prik Kaeng　น้ำพริกแกง

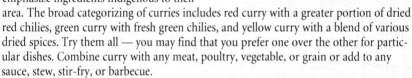

Curries of Southeast Asia are similar to the popular curries of Indian cuisine. The term curry generally defines a highly seasoned mixture of various ingredients. Making your own curry requires pounding dry and wet ingredients together to form a paste. Prepared bottled sauces and powders are good alternatives and require less time and energy to use.

Manufacturers of curry products will emphasize ingredients indigenous to their area. The broad categorizing of curries includes red curry with a greater portion of dried red chilies, green curry with fresh green chilies, and yellow curry with a blend of various dried spices. Try them all — you may find that you prefer one over the other for particular dishes. Combine curry with any meat, poultry, vegetable, or grain or add to any sauce, stew, stir-fry, or barbecue.

Prepared curry sauces and powders are available in various sized cans, jars, and bottles. Store powders in a cool, dry place and sauces in the refrigerator. Both types will keep for several months.

Dashi

(Japanese) Dashi　だし

Dashi or fish stock is a base ingredient for many traditional Japanese soups and other dishes. It is simply made from dried giant sea kelp (kombu), bonito (katsuobushi), and hot water. The first infusion of kelp and bonito produces the most flavorful dashi. This dashi is commonly used in clear soups. The second infusion is milder in flavor and all-purpose in use.

Although the most flavorful dashi is made from the best quality kelp and bonito, many home cooks are finding it easier to use instant dashi (dashi-no-moto). It comes in the form of easy dissolving granules, powder, or concentrate. It's all premeasured and ready to go — just add hot water. Use dashi in soups, marinades, sauces, dressings, and simmered dishes.

Store prepared dashi in a tightly sealed container. It will keep in the refrigerator for several days or freeze for up to a month. It is best, however, to make only as much dashi as you need, as its flavor and aroma will diminish over time. Instant dashi will keep in a cool, dry place for several months.

Fish Sauce

Yue Lo; Yu Lu 魚露
(Vietnamese) Nước Mắm

This thin, salty, amber-colored sauce is an all-purpose flavoring agent used throughout Southeast Asia and Southern China. It is such a popular ingredient that it is considered the equivalent of Chinese and Japanese soy sauce. The fermented fish extract has a distinct pungent aroma, something like soy sauce and fish, but don't let the smell throw you off — it mellows with cooking and adds a delicious, slightly salty taste to foods.

If it's not in a Thai or Vietnamese dish, fish sauce will probably be served on the side as a condiment. Add fish sauce to stews, marinades, and dipping sauces. For a traditional spicy hot condiment, combine finely sliced fresh chilies with fish sauce.

Many Southeast Asian companies produce different varieties of fish sauce, so sample small bottles to see which one you prefer. Store fish sauce in a cool, dry place for up to several months.

Galangal

(Thai) Kha ข่า

Galangal is a rhizome with a thin, translucent, pale yellow skin. It looks similar to young ginger, but galangal has thin, dark growth rings on its surface and woody pink shoots. It also comes in the form of powder or dried slices which need to be soaked before use.

Of course, fresh is best, but it is hard to find and dried products are comparable in quality. A ½-inch piece of fresh galangal is equivalent to about 1 teaspoon of the powder. Powdered and dried slices yield a stronger, more intense flavor compared to fresh which is mellower. Slice fresh galangal or use dried slices to flavor stews. Unlike ginger, galangal slices aren't eaten but are removed from finished dishes — it has a slight medicinal taste when eaten alone. Pound fresh galangal or soaked slices until smooth and add to curry blends.

Wrap fresh galangal in a paper bag and refrigerate for up to two weeks. Store dried galangal slices and powder in a cool, dry place for up to several months.

Kamaboko

(Japanese) Kamaboko かまぼこ

Have you ever been to the supermarket and seen something that resembled a long, bright pink sponge laying on a thin strip of wood? If you have, you've found kamaboko, ready-to-eat Japanese fish cake. Kamaboko is made from a mixture of pureed white fish and potato starch which is molded, colored, and steamed. It is a favorite snack food among the Japanese who eat it plain with soy sauce or with noodles in dishes like hot udon soup or cold somen salad.

The most popular type of fish cake is ita-kamaboko or planked kamaboko. The 6-inch strip rests on a thin piece of cedar which in the old days was used to impart a woodsy flavor. It remains today, as it is aesthetically pleasing and proves to be a useful cutting board. Chikuwa resembles a grilled, hollow brown tube. Natuto is easily identified by its colorful inner swirling pattern. All can be grilled, poached, or deep-fried.

Kamaboko is available in the refrigerated section of Asian markets. Check the package for storage information and expiration date. After opening, it will keep for a week.

Kimchee

Hon Sig Yim Choy; Han Shih Yen Tsai
(Korean) 김치   韓式腌菜

No Korean meal is complete without kimchee, a pickled vegetable condiment that is garlicky, salty, and spicy hot. It is typically made with napa cabbage, but an assortment of vegetables, such as turnips, watercress, mustard greens, and onions are also used.

Just one look and one whiff will make you think twice about eating kimchee. The pickled vegetables are laced with bright red flecks of chili and have a pungent odor, but they taste wonderful.

Every Korean household has at least one favorite family recipe to make kimchee, but as with Western pickling and preserving, making kimchee at home takes time. Lucky for us, jars of hot, medium, and, mild kimchee are available in the refrigerated section of many supermarkets. Check the jar for storage information and expiration date. After opening, it will keep for up to a month.

Lemongrass

Heung Mao; Hsiang Mao 香茅
(Thai) Takrai ตะไคร้

Lemongrass looks like a very long, woody green onion that's pale yellow-green in color. When cooked, lemongrass imparts a delicate lemony flavor and aroma. It is a classic ingredient in many Southeast Asian countries including Indonesia, Malaysia, Thailand, and Vietnam.

Only the moist portion of lemongrass, the bottom 6-inches, is suitable for cooking. Discard the top and remove the fibrous layer on the bottom portion if it looks dry. Use lemongrass to flavor soups, stews, curries, and stir-fries. For soups, gently crush the stalk and add it whole; slice, dice, or mince it for other cooking. When used whole or in large pieces, it is best to remove lemongrass before serving as it tends to become stringy during cooking. When using dried lemongrass, soak it in warm water until softened. If lemongrass is not available, substitute 1 teaspoon fresh lemon peel for one stalk lemongrass.

Fresh and dried lemongrass are available in Asian markets. Wrap fresh lemongrass in paper towels and refrigerate for up to two weeks or freeze for up to a month.

Mirin

Yut Boon Tim Mike Tziu;
Jih Pen Tien Mi Chiu 日本甜米酒
(Japanese) Mirin みりん

Mirin is an essential seasoning ingredient in Japanese cooking; it gives teriyaki sauce and sushi rice their sweet taste and shiny glaze. Mirin, or sweet cooking rice wine, is made from the fermentation of glutinous rice and a bit of sugar for sweetening. It is a thin, light golden seasoning liquid with an average 12 percent alcohol content. Although it is classified as a wine, mirin is not used for drinking, but is used primarily to flavor foods leaving a light sweet taste.

There are two types of mirin. Hon-mirin, also called sweet sake, is a naturally brewed wine. Aji-mirin is mirin made with the addition of salt and corn syrup. Both can be used interchangeably and can be used in almost any dish. During cooking, the alcohol evaporates leaving a sweet, subtle wine taste. Add mirin to teriyaki sauce, dressings, marinades, dipping sauces, sukiyaki, and other simmered Japanese dishes.

Store mirin in a cool, dry place. It will keep for several months.

Miso

Yut Boon Tzee Mike So;
Jih Pen Chih Mi Su 日本之米素
(Japanese) Miso みそ

Protein-rich and appealing because of its taste and aroma, miso is one of the staples in the Japanese diet. There are several types of miso which are made from the same basic ingredients of crushed soy beans and barley, rice, or wheat. The mixture is fermented over a period of several months to several years, producing thick, rich, pungent pastes, each with a different aroma, flavor, color, and consistency.

Westerners are probably most familiar with traditional Japanese miso soup. All miso pastes are salty tasting, but white and yellow pastes are sweeter, milder tasting, and best to use as an all-purpose miso for dressings, dips, soups, and grilled foods. Red and brown miso pastes are more savory and add rich flavors to stews and soups. When adding miso to a dish, mix it with some of the liquid called for in the recipe to ensure that it dissolves completely.

Miso is available packaged in bags, tubs, tubes, and jars in the refrigerated section of Asian markets. After opening, all types will keep for several months, but will lose flavor over time.

Palm Sugar

(Thai) Nam Tan Peep น้ำตาลมะพร้าว

In Western cooking, cane sugar sweetens foods; in Southeast Asia, palm sugar is the basic sweetener. To obtain palm sugar, sap is tapped from various palm trees, collected, and boiled down to a thick syrup which is then poured into bamboo pipe molds. The thick, sticky bamboo-shaped cakes are maple brown to deep brown in color and coarse and crumbly in texture. Palm sugar adds a smooth, rich sweetness to foods.

Palm sugar, also known as coconut sugar, is mainly used to balance strong flavors. It compliments spicy, salty, and sour tastes which are common flavors in Southeast Asian cuisines. Although the flavor will not be as rich or intense, dark brown sugar can be substituted for palm sugar.

Palm sugar is available in plastic packages. Transfer the contents of an opened package to a tightly sealed container and store in a cool, dry place. It will keep for several months.

Panko

Yut Boon Tzee Min Bao Hong;
Jih Pen Chih Mien Bao Kang 日本之麵包糠
(Japanese) Panko パン粉

Panko is the name for Japanese-style bread crumbs. These dried, toasted flakes are larger and coarser than Western-style bread crumbs. They are used to give deep-fried foods, such as tonkatsu, deep-fried Japanese pork cutlet, a crunchy coating.

Unlike some batter or bread crumb-coated foods, panko does not taste greasy after frying; it retains its crisp texture even after standing. Use panko as you would bread crumbs. Toss panko with your favorite seasoning and sprinkle over casseroles for a different look and texture.

Panko is available in various sized plastic bags. Transfer the contents of an opened package to a self-sealing plastic bag and store in a cool, dry place. It will keep for several months.

Pressed Bean Curd

Dou Fu Gon; Tou Fu Kan 豆腐乾
(Japanese) Kata-Toufu 堅豆腐

Pressed bean curd is similar to fresh bean curd, but more whey (liquid) has been removed from the coagulated mixture to make a curd which is very firm and compact. It is usually sold as flat square cakes or as 1-inch thick bricks. Pressed bean curd is also available marinated with different seasonings including soy sauce, star anise, Chinese five-spice, and sesame oil. Colors range from milky white to deep brown.

Pressed bean curd is somewhat chewy and meat-like in texture, making it a good choice for vegetarian dishes. When using plain pressed bean curd, simmer it with your favorite seasonings before eating. Cut seasoned cakes into thin strips and add them to soups and salads for added flavor and texture.

Pressed bean curd is available in plastic packages in the refrigerated section of Asian markets. Check the package for storage information and expiration date. After opening, it will keep for a week.

Sake

Yut Boon Tzee Mike Tziu;
Jih Pen Chih Mi Chiu 日本之米酒
(Japanese) Nihonshu 日本酒

Although in Japan the word sake is a generic term used to describe all alcoholic beverages, most people think of sake as the potent rice wine which holds greatest honor in Japanese culture. As Japan's national beverage, sake is drunk at religious ceremonies, weddings, festivals, on holidays, and special occasions.

Sake has a clean, lightly sweet, flowery taste. As a beverage, sake is served warm or cold. To warm sake, pour into a small serving bottle and place in a hot water bath. Sake is also used as a flavoring ingredient in cooking. It adds a rich flavor and glossy sheen to finished dishes. Use sake in marinades to tenderize meats or to remove off odors and fishy tastes.

Sake is available in a variety of sizes and decorative bottles. Store an unopened bottle in a cool, dry place. Unlike wine, sake does not need to be aged; it tastes best when used within several months of purchase.

Seaweed

Tzee Choy; Tzi Tsai 紫菜
(Japanese) Kaisou 海草

Two types of dried seaweed are commonly used in Japanese cooking: deep green sheets (nori) used to wrap sushi and the olive-brown giant sea kelp (kombu) used to make dashi. Both seaweeds are harvested from the sea, washed, dried, seasoned, and packaged. In Chinese cuisine, seaweed is used mainly in soups.

To make rolled sushi, buy toasted nori (yaki-nori) or toast plain sheets yourself. Carefully wave a sheet of nori over a stove burner until it turns crisp and bright green; be careful not to burn the delicate sheet. Cut it into the desired size, place shiny side down, and wrap rice and desired filling inside. Slightly wet end of nori to seal. Nori sheets are also available seasoned (ajitsuke nori) with hot spices and teriyaki flavors. When using kombu to make traditional Japanese dashi, gently wipe the surface with a damp cloth, but don't scrape or wash off the flavorful white powder.

Seaweed is available in cans, jars, and plastic packages. Transfer the contents of an opened package to a self-sealing plastic bag. Store seaweed in a cool, dry place for up to several months.

Tamarind

Law Mong Tzee Dic Guor Sut;
Lo Wang Tzi Ti Kuo Shih 羅望子的果實
(Thai) Som Ma Kham มะขามเปียก

Tamarind provides the fruity sour flavor characteristic of Southeast Asian curries, chutneys, soups, and stews. The dusty brown pod from the tamarind tree has a dark brown pulp inside which is fibrous, sticky, and clings to several seeds. Processed tamarind paste is more commonly available in brick form, composed of pulp with or without seeds. The paste is thick, purple-brown in color with a taste like sour prunes. Tamarind concentrate and powder are also available.

When a recipe calls for tamarind liquid, combine ½ cup hot water and 2½ tablespoons tamarind paste. Let soak until softened. Knead the pulp from the seeds and strain the liquid through a fine sieve before using. Use the liquid in marinades, sauces, and braised dishes. Follow package directions when using tamarind concentrate and powder.

Store pods and opened packages of paste and powder in plastic bags and keep in a cool, dry place. Refrigerate opened jars of concentrate. All types of tamarind will keep for several months.

Teriyaki Sauce

Shao Kao Chiang 日式燒烤醬
(Japanese) Teriyaki-Tare 照り焼きたれ

Teriyaki sauce is one of the most delicious culinary exports to come from Japan. It has a savory, sweet flavor that goes well with any barbecued or grilled meat, poultry, fish, or shellfish. Traditionally made from equal portions of soy sauce and mirin, today's teriyaki sauce may include additional ingredients such as pineapple juice, sake, brown sugar, ginger, and garlic.

When you don't have time to make your own teriyaki sauce, use a bottle of prepared teriyaki sauce. Convenient and flavorful, it is perfect for basting, glazing, marinating, and stir-frying. Just stir-fry some meat and vegetables, add a few tablespoons of the sauce, and you've got an instant meal.

Refrigerate prepared teriyaki sauce after opening. It will keep for several months.

Thai Sweet Basil

Tai Guok Tim Law Log;
Tai Kuo Tien Lo Le 泰國甜羅勒
(Thai) Bai Horapa ใบกะเพรา

For those of you who enjoy the slightly strong, yet sweet lingering flavor of anise, you must try this fresh herb. It plays an important role in Thai and Vietnamese cuisines. Thai sweet basil has bright green leaves with purplish green stems and flowers. It has an aromatic anise fragrance and flavor.

Use Thai sweet basil as you would other fresh herbs. Toss whole leaves into salads or add to stir-fried dishes. Stack a few whole leaves on top of each other and roll into a bundle. Turn the bundle sideways and thinly slice to make fine shreds. Use shreds to garnish soups and sauces. Pound chopped basil into curry paste, or serve whole trimmed bunches as an accompaniment to Vietnamese noodle soup. Just pluck the leaves from the stem and drop them into the fragrant hot broth.

To store Thai sweet basil, place stem ends in a glass of water, cover with a plastic bag, and refrigerate. It will keep for several days, but it is best when used the day of purchase.

Preparing Fresh Coconut Cream and Milk

Coconuts are commonly used throughout Southeast Asia in curries, stews, and desserts. Choose fresh coconuts that are free of cracks and mold. Shake the coconut; it should sound full and feel heavy. Pierce the eyes of the coconut and drain the water into a bowl. The coconut water should taste sweet. Blend it into refreshing tropical drinks or drink as is. Discard the water and the coconut if the water tastes sour or has a foul odor.

Hold the coconut in one hand with the eyes facing up. Firmly hit the coconut about an inch below the eyes with a hammer. Rotate the coconut and continue hitting until it cracks open. Break it into smaller pieces. Separate the shell from the tender white meat and discard.

Cut the meat into small pieces and finely chop in a food processor. Add a cup of hot water and blend well. Place the coconut mixture in a fine sieve and firmly press to obtain the thick, creamy, rich coconut cream. Return the grated coconut mixture to the food processor and add another cup of hot water. Process again until well blended. Place the sieve over another bowl and firmly press the mixture to remove the thinner coconut milk. You can repeat this process several times, but after each pressing, the milk will become thinner and more diluted.

Transfer the cream and milk to tightly sealed containers and refrigerate immediately. Both liquids are best used the day they are made but can be refrigerated for up to two days or frozen for up to several weeks.

Wasabi

Yut Boon Gai Laut; Jih Pen Chieh La日本芥辣
(Japanese) Wasabi わさび

If you've eaten sashimi or sushi, you've probably tasted wasabi, one of the strongest spices used in Japanese cooking. Served as a paste, the pale green color looks cool and refreshing, but don't let that fool you. Wasabi is a fiery hot Japanese horseradish, and a little goes a long way. Fresh wasabi root is available in Asian markets, but wasabi powders and prepared wasabi paste are more commonly used in Japanese kitchens.

To mix the powder into a paste, blend in enough water to make a thick creamy mixture. Let it stand for at least 10 minutes before serving. One tablespoon of powder makes enough paste to serve four people as a condiment. When eating sushi and sashimi, each person adds wasabi to taste to his bowl of soy sauce.

A variety of powder-filled tins and tubes of pastes are available. Store powder in a cool, dry place for up to several months. Refrigerate opened tubes of paste and use as soon as possible as the flavor dissipates over time.

Wheat Noodles

Min Tiu; Mien Tiao 麵條
(Japanese) Chuukamen 中華麵

Soba, udon, and somen are three of Japan's most popular noodles. They not only differ in looks, but vary greatly in flavor and texture, allowing the cook to make endless variations with hot and cold noodle dishes.

Fat chewy udon noodles and delicate thread-like somen noodles are made from wheat flour. Both are white in color, but sometimes somen is colored: green (cha somen) is tinted with green tea; red (ume somen) is tinted with red perilla oil; and yellow (tamago somen) is tinted with egg yolk.

Soba, or buckwheat noodles, are made from a combination of buckwheat flour and wheat flour. They are light tan in color and have a wonderful earthy flavor. A green tea variety (cha soba) has an olive-green color and a delicate tea flavor.

Dried and fresh wheat noodles are available in plastic packages. Check the package for storage information and expiration date. Cook wheat noodles according to the package directions.

Asian Ingredient Sources

Asian Condiments and Spices
14455 Don Julian Road
City of Industry, CA 91746
(818) 336-3886   Mail Order

JFC International Incorporated
540 Forbes Boulevard
South San Francisco, CA 94080
(415) 871-1660   Mail Order

Woks 'N Things
2234 South Wentworth Avenue
Chicago, IL 60616
(312) 842-0701

Uwajimaya
519 Sixth Avenue, South
Seattle, WA 98104
(206) 624-6248   Mail Order

China Bowl Trading Company
P.O. Box 454
Westport, CT 06880
(203) 222-0381   Mail Order

Mee Wah Lung
608 "H" Street, Northwest
Washington, D.C. 20001
(202) 737-0968

The Oriental Pantry
423 Great Road
Acton, MA 01720
(800) 828-0368   Mail Order

Kam Man Food Products
200 Canal Street
New York, NY 10013
(212) 571-0330   Mail Order

Orient Delight Market
865 East El Camino Real
Mountain View, CA 94040
(415) 969-4288   Mail Order

Oriental Food Market
2801 West Howard Street
Chicago, IL 60645
(312) 274-2826   Mail Order

DeWildt Imports
Fox Gap Road, R.D. #3
Bangor, PA 18013
(800) 338-3433   Mail Order

Kwong On Lung Company
922 South San Pedro Street
Los Angeles, CA 90015
(213) 628-1069

For information on authentic Chinese sauces, contact:
Lee Kum Kee

304 S. Date Avenue
Alhambra, CA 91803 (USA)
(818) 282-0337
(800) 654-5082
(818) 282-3425 (FAX)

2-4 Dai Fat Street
Tai Po Ind. Est.
Hong Kong.
(852) 660 3600
(852) 665 8005 (FAX)

Index

A

agar agar	66
anise, star	17, 20
apple pear	47
Asian eggplant	47
Asian pear	47

B

baby bok choy	48
baby corn	59
baby ginger	52
bamboo shoots	59
barbecue sauce	23
basil, Thai sweet	87
basmati rice	38
bean curd,	
fermented	25
fresh	76, 77
pressed	84
bean curd puffs	76
bean curd sheets	77
bean curd sticks	77
bean sprouts	48
bean thread noodles	36
beans, yard long	43, 56
Beijing (Peking)	32
black bean sauce	23
black fungus	21, 60
black mushrooms, dried	21, 60
black vinegar	66
bok choy	43, 48
bonito	78, 79
broccoli, Chinese	43, 49
brown bean sauce	24
brown slab sugar	17

C

cabbage, napa	54, 62, 81
candies, Chinese New Year	67
celery cabbage	54
chee hou sauce	26
chili oil	24
chili paste	25
chili peppers	24, 25, 49, 70
Chinatown	5, 67
Chinese black mushrooms	21, 60
Chinese broccoli	43, 49
Chinese chives	50
Chinese eggplant	47
Chinese five-spice	17
Chinese grapefruit	54
Chinese hot mustard	18
Chinese jujubes	21
Chinese New Year	53, 54, 67
Chinese New Year candies	53, 67
Chinese okra	43, 50
Chinese parsley	51
Chinese sausage	67
Chinese turnips	43, 51, 62, 81
Chinkiang vinegar	66
chips, shrimp	71
chives, Chinese	50
choy, bok	43, 48
cilantro	43, 51
cloud ear	60
coconut,	
cream	78, 87
fresh	67, 78, 87
milk	39, 78, 87
cooking techniques, basic	12-13
corn, baby	59
cuisine, Chinese regional	32-33
curry	79
cutting techniques, basic	10

D

daikon	51
dark soy sauce	31
dashi	78, 79, 85
dim sum	33, 37, 42, 57
dried black mushrooms	21, 60
dried lily buds	21
dried lotus leaves	68
dried lychee	69
dried orange peel	20
dried red chilies	24, 25, 49,
dried rice noodles	40
dried shrimp	71
dried tangerine peel	17, 20, 21
duck eggs	68
duck sauce	27

E

egg noodles	36
egg roll wrappers	37, 41
eggplant, Asian	47
eggs, duck	68
enoki mushrooms	53
equipment, basic	8-9

F

fermented bean curd	25
fermented black beans	19, 23
fish sauce	80
five-spice, Chinese	17

Index

flour,
    glutinous rice 37
    rice 37, 40, 41, 57
flowering chives 50
fungus,
    black 21, 60
    white 63

G

galangal 80
ginger,
    fresh 21, 52, 70
    preserved 61
ginseng 21, 73
glutinous rice 37, 38, 39, 82
glutinous rice flour 37
grapefruit, Chinese 54
green chives 50
Guangzhou (Canton) 33

H

herbs, Chinese medicinal 21, 73
hoisin sauce 26
hot mustard, Chinese 18
Hunan 33
hundred year old duck eggs 68

J

Japanese eggplant 47
Japanese turnips 51, 62, 81
jasmine rice 38
jicama 52
jujubes, Chinese 21

K

kamaboko 81
kimchee 51, 81
kumquat 53, 67

L

lemongrass 21, 82
lily buds, dried 21
long-grain rice 37, 38, 39
lotus leaves, dried 68
lychee,
    fresh and canned 21, 61
    dried 69

M

medicinal herbs, Chinese 21, 73
medium-grain rice 38, 39
melon, winter 43, 56, 67, 70
mirin 82, 86
miso 83
mung bean sprouts 48
mushrooms,

canned 62
    dried 21, 60
    fresh 53
mustard, Chinese hot 18

N

napa cabbage 54, 62, 81
noodles,
    bean thread (cellophane) 36
    dried rice 40
    egg 36
    fresh rice 40
    wheat 88

O

oil,
    chili 24
    peanut 69
    sesame 28
okra, Chinese 43, 50
orange peel, dried 20
oyster-flavored sauce 26
oyster mushrooms 53

P

palm sugar 39, 83
panko 84
parsley, Chinese 51
peanut oil 69
pear, Asian 47
peas, snow 43, 55
peel, dried tangerine 17, 20, 21
peel, dried orange 20
peppers, chili 49
peppercorns, Sichuan 17, 19
plum sauce 27
pomelo 54
preparation techniques, basic 11
preserved black beans 19, 23
preserved ginger 61
preserved vegetables, Sichuan 62
pressed bean curd 84

R

radish, giant white 51, 62, 81
reduced sodium soy sauce 30
red vinegar 66
rice,
    glutinous 37, 38, 39, 82
    long-grain 37, 38, 39
    medium-grain 38, 39
    short-grain 38, 39
rice crusts (or cakes) 39
rice flour 37, 40, 41, 57

Index

rice noodles,
   dried   40
   fresh   40
rice papers   41
rice vinegar   27, 66
rice wine   28, 82, 85, 86
rock sugar (or candy)   18
root, taro   55

S

sake   28, 82, 85, 86
salted black beans   19, 23
salted duck eggs   68
satay sauce   23
sausage, Chinese   67
seaweed   85
seed companies   43
seeds, sesame   70
sesame oil   28
sesame paste   29
sesame seeds   29, 70
Shanghai   33
Shanghai baby bok choy   48
Shao Hsing wine   28
shiitake mushrooms   21, 53, 60
shoots, bamboo   59
short-grain rice   38, 39
shrimp chips   71
shrimp, dried   71
shrimp sauce   29
Sichuan   33
Sichuan peppercorns   17, 19
Sichuan preserved vegetables   62
snow peas   43, 55
soba   88
somen   88
sources, Asian ingredient   89
soy beans   23, 24, 26, 30, 32, 76, 77, 83
soy bean sprouts   48
soy sauce   30-31, 86
spring roll wrappers   37, 41
sprouts, bean   48
star anise   17, 20
starch,
   tapioca   42
   wheat   42, 57
straw mushrooms   62
sticky rice   39
sugar,
   brown slab   17
   palm   39, 83

rock   18
sushi   27, 38, 82, 85, 88
sweet basil, Thai   87
sweet bean sauce   32
sweet rice   39

T

tamarind   86
tangerine peel, dried   17, 20, 21
tapioca pearls   42
tapioca starch   42
taro root   55
tea   72-73
teriyaki sauce   82, 86
Thai eggplant   47
Thai sweet basil   87
thin soy sauce   31
thousand year old duck eggs   68
tools, basic   8-9
tree ear   60
turnips, Chinese and Japanese   43, 51

U

udon   88

V

vegetables, Sichuan preserved   62
vegetables, growing   43
vinegar, rice   27, 66

W

wasabi   18, 88
water chestnuts   63, 67
wheat noodles   88
wheat starch   42, 57
white fungus   63
wine, rice   28, 82, 85, 86
winter melon   43, 56, 67, 70
wonton wrappers   37, 43
wood ear   60
wrappers,
   egg roll   37, 41
   spring roll   37, 41
   wonton   37, 43

Y

yard long beans   43, 56
yellow chives   50
yin and yang   21, 70
young corn   59
young ginger   52, 61

Martin Yan's Cutlery Collection :

Peking Slicer (left)
All-Purpose Chinese Chef Knife (top)
Handy Vegetable Knife (middle)
Paring Knife (bottom)

Selected Gourmet Merchandise

YanCanCook

To show our appreciation we are offering you the following items at a special price.

Quantity		Price/ea.	Shipping/ea.
_____ Copy(s) THE WELL-SEASONED WOK cookbook		14.00	2.00
_____ Copy(s) EVERYBODY'S WOKKING cookbook		14.00	2.00
_____ Copy(s) A WOK FOR ALL SEASONS cookbook		13.00	2.00
_____ Copy(s) MARTIN YAN, THE CHINESE CHEF cookbook		12.00	2.00
_____ Copy(s) THE YAN CAN COOK BOOK cookbook		12.00	2.00
_____ Copy(s) SIMPLE GUIDE TO CHINESE INGREDIENTS...		4.00	1.00
_____ MARTIN YAN'S ALL-PURPOSE CHINESE CHEF KNIFE		45.00	3.00
_____ MARTIN YAN'S HANDY VEGETABLE KNIFE		35.00	3.00
_____ MARTIN YAN'S PEKING SLICER		25.00	2.00
_____ MARTIN YAN'S PARING KNIFE		10.00	2.00

Subtotal $ _____

California residents add applicable local Sales Tax $ _____

(Alaska, Hawaii and Canada residents add $3.00 <u>extra</u> for shipping) $ _____

Total Amount $ _____

❏ Check   ❏ Money Order   ❏ Visa   ❏ MasterCard
(Make checks payable to: **Yan Can Cook, Inc.**)

Card #_____ Exp. Date_____

Signature_____

Name_____

Address _____ Apt. #_____

City_____State_____Zip_____

Phone #   (_____)_____

Please allow approximately two to four (2-4) weeks for delivery.
Yan Can Cook, Inc. P.O. Box 4755 Foster City, CA 94404
Phone: 415-341-5133 • Fax: 415-341-5191